AF474021

ORGANIC DESIGN

Products Inspired by Nature

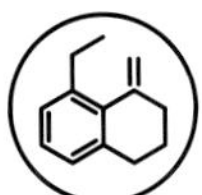

SendPoints

ORGANIC DESIGN—Products Inspired by Nature

EDITED & PUBLISHED BY SendPoints Publishing Co., Ltd.
PUBLISHER: Lin Gengli
PUBLISHING DIRECTOR: Lin Shijian
CHIEF EDITOR: Lin Shijian
EXECUTIVE EDITOR: Coco Xian,Weiji Li
ART DIRECTOR: He Wanling
EXECUTIVE ART EDITOR: Waikin Ho
PROOFREADING: Timothy Kennett

REGISTERED ADDRESS: Room 15A Block 9 Tsui Chuk Garden, Wong Tai Sin, Kowloon, Hong Kong
TEL: +852-35832323 / **FAX:** +852-35832448
OFFICE ADDRESS: 7F, 9th Anning Street, Jinshazhou, Baiyun District, Guangzhou, China
TEL: +86-20-89095121 / **FAX:** +86-20-89095206
BEIJING OFFICE: Room 107, Floor 1, Xiyingfang Alley, Ande Road, Dongcheng District, Beijing, China
TEL: +86-10-84139071 / **FAX:** +86-10-84139071
SHANGHAI OFFICE: Room 307, Building 1, Hong Qiang Creative Zhabei District, Shanghai, China
TEL: +86-21-63523469 / **FAX:** +86-21-63523469

SALES MANAGER: Sissi
TEL: +86-20-81007895
EMAIL: overseas01@sendpoints.cn
WEBSITE: www.sendpoints.cn / www.spbooks.cn

ISBN 978-988-14703-5-5

Printed and bound in China

This book is dedicated to nature,
the source of inspiration for all of its contents.

Carlos Jiménez Pérez
Co-founder of the photoAlquimia studio
Biologist, Nature photographer, Designer

" Every day it seems more probable that nature-inspired design is the design of the future. "

PREFACE

What source of inspiration could lead us into a new era of totally fresh and innovative product designs that improve mankind's quality of life, objects that are simple yet sophisticated, elegant, intelligent and respectful of our planet?

It is quite possible that we can find the answer in nature, the first design studio founded on planet Earth. Over 3.8 billion years of evolution, nature has been designing and improving infinite solutions, all aimed towards a single goal: to enable and sustain life on the planet. The rich diversity of our planet contains an endless number of solutions to structural problems, in terms of energy and functionality, all tested and improved over millions of years. It seems logical to think that it would be easier to take advantage of the vast archive of information that nature offers us than to exploit all of its resources uncontrollably. The beauty of nature is present in the collective conscious and unconscious of all mankind, and has been since the beginning of time. In nature we can find all kinds of patterns and combinations of shapes, colors and textures. These fascinating models serve as an inexhaustible source of inspiration for designers and artists.

Biomimicry, also known as biomimetics, refers to a field of knowledge that uses natural wisdom as its inspiration, or source of imitation, in order to resolve certain human problems that nature has already solved thousands of years earlier. In product design, biomimicry is a powerful tool and an endless source of inspiration, bound by the principles of life itself, trying to imitate the shapes, textures or functions of living organisms in order to reach optimal design solutions. In turn, living organisms are integrated into natural ecosystems following closed cycles of matter and energy, which in turn integrate into a greater planetary system, creating the biosphere. In nature's economy, waste is converted into raw material to create anew, and the sun as an energy source is clean and inexhaustible. Inspiration and imitation of nature at a higher level, whether it be the functionality of ecosystems or the relationships between them, can be very useful in other areas of knowledge such as economy, politics or philosophy. Understanding the basic principles of life through biomimicry is essential to the construction of production systems that are harmoniously integrated with nature's systems.

THE PRESENT...

One might think that biomimicry is a current trend in product design that only developed in recent years. In actuality, mankind has been totally bound to nature since its origin, and has needed to observe and learn from nature in order to ensure its own survival and evolution. Much of human knowledge draws from the observation and imitation of nature. We can find indigenous communities that have been practicing biomimicry in their lifestyles for thousands of years.

Since the Industrial Revolution, approximately 200 years ago, biomimicry has fallen into a deep sleep, in contrast to the high-speed progress of human society. In the last century, humans have expanded exponentially, both in terms of numbers and of their exploitation of territories. There are too many of us and our current ways of life have become unsustainable in the context of nature's cycles. We find ourselves in ecological crisis, pushing nature's systems to the limits of tolerance.

Luckily, the human race appears to be at a point of inflection, both intellectually and philosophically. A change is happening in our thoughts regarding our relationship with nature, and we are moving towards seeing it as a source of wisdom and a guarantor of our future, rather than as a source of endlessly exploited resources. Today, biomimicry is starting to receive global recognition. More and more engineers, designers and architects are inspired by natural processes to develop designs that improve human's quality of life and the planet.

THE FUTURE...

The design projects that we find in this book either imitate or were inspired by nature in terms of their shape, texture or function. Product design of this kind is currently serving as a global messenger for this new and revolutionary way of thinking, and in the near future will facilitate changes in production systems such that they will become more sustainable and compatible with life. A natural design that inspires us today as designers, though it was created thousands of years ago, patiently reveals itself when it is observed as elegant, modern and innovative, and arguably timeless and beyond trends.

Thanks to our current era of communication and maximum specialization in fields of knowledge, global networks are being created for specialists who participate in complex design projects. In the field of biomimicry, there are already working networks that operate globally on specific design projects. In the Age of Aquarius we've just entered, we aim to begin an era of sustainability, which is why biomimicry emerges as a radical new approach to product design, engineering, architecture and art.

In the following pages you will be able to enjoy the work of numerous designers from around the globe, all of whom have become aware, or rather become convinced, that humanity's future resides in the re-evolution of biomimicry, which holds the key to sustainable long-term development. We still have much to learn from nature: new shapes, materials and functions, all integrated in closed cycles of matter and energy, free of waste, employing quality raw materials, all giving us insight into incredible designs that are yet to be imagined.

Every day it seems more probable that nature-inspired design is the design of the future.

CATALOG

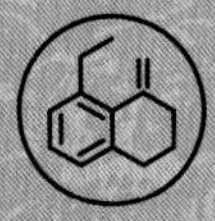

Form

P010–P169

Texture

P170–P243

Function

P244–P269

Form

Nature-inspired forms, which have a long history as an approach to design, endow a product with life and fun. They are a result of many generations' observation and study of nature. The product designs in this chapter were developed either with nature as the motivation, or with nature as the optimal solution for satisfying specific needs. They all offer an invaluable, unusual living experience.

Soytun

Studio photoAlquimia

Designer Carlos Jiménez, Pilar Balsalobre

Manufactured with enameled stoneware, Soytun is a ceramic piece designed to use to taste raw fish such as sashimi, sushi, tartar, etc., which are increasingly popular. This design serves to contain the soy sauce and the spicy mustard (wasabi), with a section for resting the chopsticks. The packaging design was inspired by the old cardboard boxes of natural history museums, which in Victorian times were used to hold zoological and botanical specimens. The gift box is produced entirely from recycled cardboard, making it a singular example of eco-packaging.

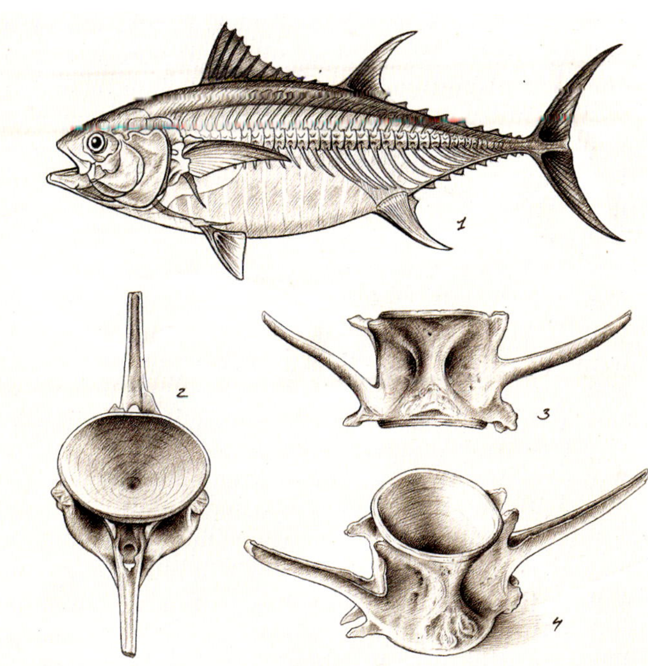
1
2
3
4
1. Esqueleto óseo de Atún rojo. 2,3,4. Diferentes vistas de una vértebra
Loc. Los Caños de Meca (Cádiz) España

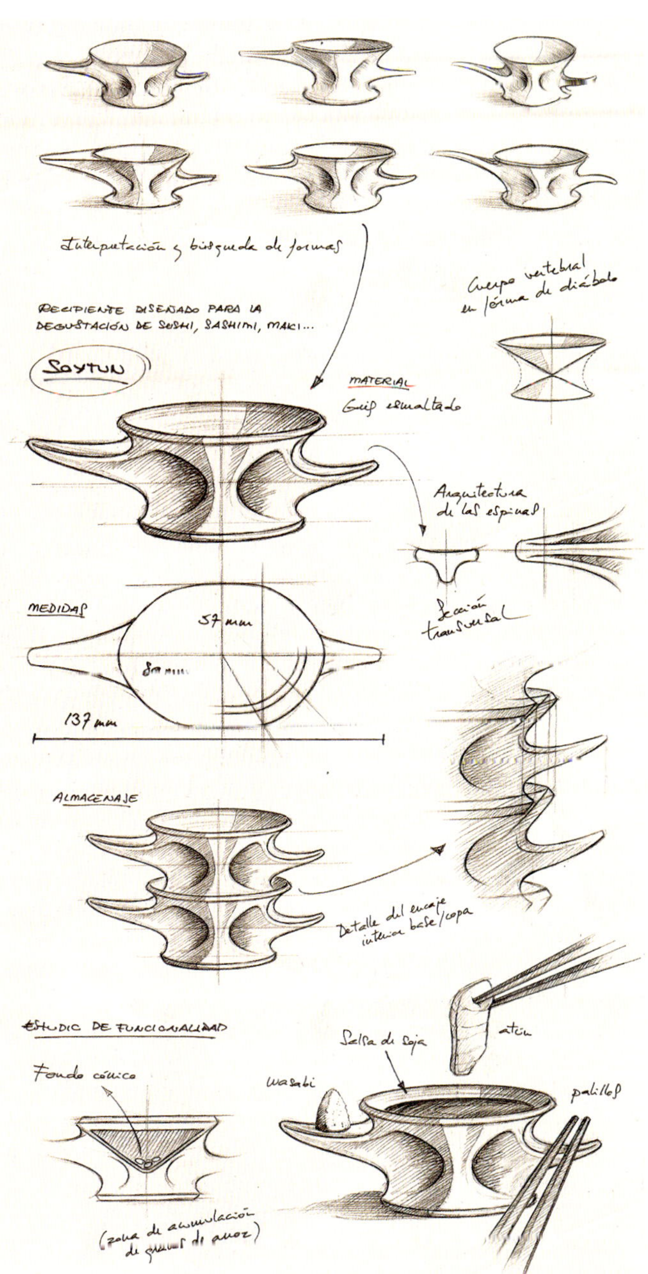
Interpretación y búsqueda de formas
Cuerpo vertebral en forma de diábolo
Recipiente diseñado para la degustación de sushi, sashimi, maki...
SOYTUN
Material
Gres esmaltado
Arquitectura de las espinas
Sección transversal
Medidas
57 mm
80 mm
137 mm
Almacenaje
Detalle del encaje interior base/copa
Estudio de funcionalidad
Fondo cónico
(zona de acumulación de granos de arroz)
Salsa de soja
atún
wasabi
palillos

by photoAlquimia
N.005
NATURA IMITATIS

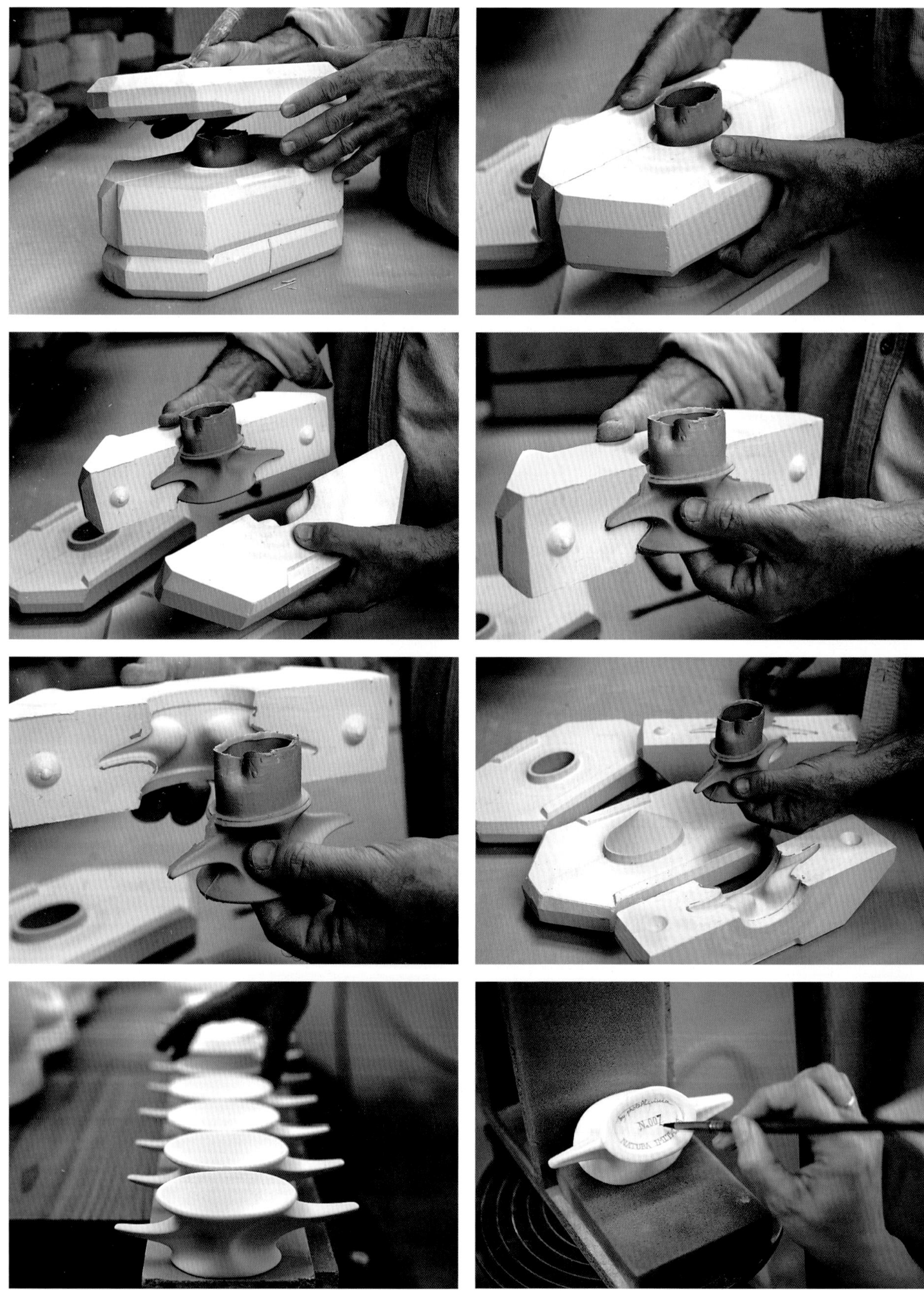
N.007

··· Interview with photoAlquimia ···

1. What do you think about the relationship between biomimetics and product design?

>>At the photoAlquimia studio we started to apply the fundamentals of biomimicry to various design projects for informative exhibits about nature and its relationship with humans. Our background in biomimicry led us to design a nature-inspired product line called "NATURA IMITATIS" (imitate nature). Soytun belongs to this collection of functional designs. We are convinced that biomimicry is a limitless tool for developing products that are innovative in terms of functionality, aesthetics and sustainability. It's pleasing to see that every day these designs are becoming more understood and appreciated globally.

2. What do you value the most in your creative life? How do you make use of it?

>>What we value the most in the creative process is enthusiasm for the project and the excitement generated in the early phases of a new design, which is an adventure charged with mystery because of all the unexpected surprises along the way.
For photoAlquimia, biomimicry, tradition, art, craft and new technologies are the fundamental ingredients that inform the conceptual structure of our projects. After a long and arduous process of simplification, our products are transformed into simple designs, endowed with their own unique stories, that invite users to reflect or contemplate.

3. Is there an interesting story behind the creation that you would like to share with us?

>>Some time ago, while working on a design project whose protagonist was the sea, we walked along a beach in southern Spain, collecting and studying objects that the waves brought to the shore. We found a huge fishbone. The shape of its neck fascinated us, for we saw in it a great work of natural engineering and we saw the first glimmerings of inspiration for a new design. We weren't sure if it was a chance find or a gift from the sea. The Soytun project, therefore, comes with a special edition booklet called *The Gift from the Sea*, which presents the entire story from inspiration and artisanal production to packaging design.

Biophilia

Studio Stoft

The Biophilia collection consists of four vessels in stoneware, porcelain and earthenware, each symbolizing a step in a plant's growing process. The stoneware bowl Capsula symbolizes the protective seedpod from which a life begins. Embraced by this coarse stoneware, the porcelain vase Petalis sprouts. The vase then branches out, forming the pitcher Truncus. At the very top rests the small earthenware vase Spore waiting to take root elsewhere by also functioning as a small vase for seedlings.

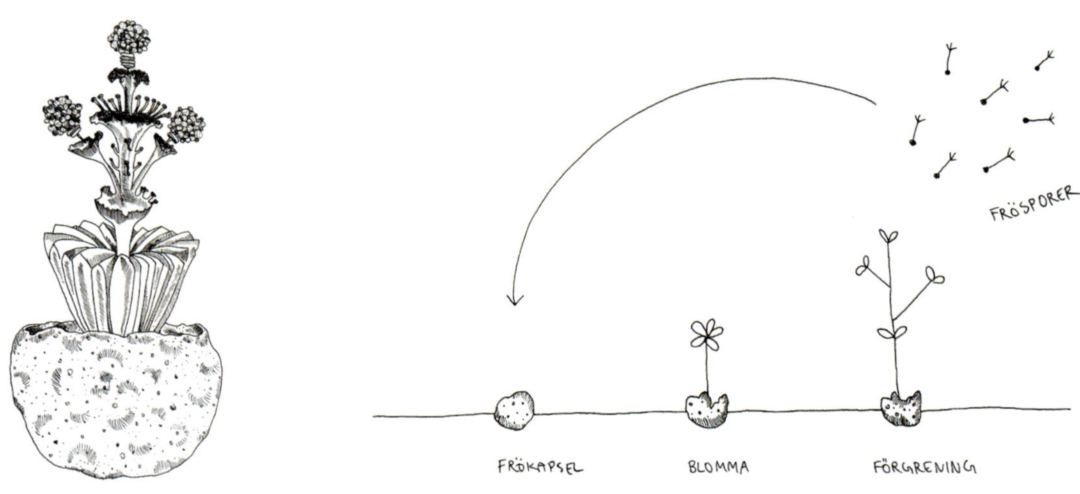

… Interview with Stoft …

1. Do you often take inspiration from nature?

>>Yes, we believe there's a lot of inspiration to be found in how nature is shaped and formed. Nature has taken its form in a long and slow process that allows things to be what they are, not by following any particular set of rules. In our projects we try to follow this way of thinking and let the products take shape throughout the design process.

2. How did you think of using four separate pieces to represent your inspiration? Is there particular consideration of the material choices?

>>With our Biophilia collection we took inspiration from the different stages in a plant's life, from seedpod to stalk, flower and spore. So having four pieces was a natural outcome. The material follows the same intention of presenting the plant as the inspiration, for example the seedpod in rough stoneware and the flower in thin porcelain.

3. Does this final product meet your expectations? What do you think is most meaningful in this project?

>>The final product is a part of the process so we were not expecting any particular outcome when we started, but we are very happy with the final result. The most meaningful part of the project has been letting the material become an integral part of the design, allowing both the visual and tactile attributes to speak for the product.

4. Is this design mass-produced or customizable?

>>This collection is locally handmade in stoneware, porcelain and earthenware, but can be made in larger quantities.

5. Is there an interesting story behind this cooperation that you would like to share with us?

>>The project is a part of the exhibition "The new map" which was initiated by Jenny Nordberg. It's a project that aims to show that local production is still possible and can be developed by pairing 24 designers with 24 manufacturers in the region of Scania in the south of Sweden. The project has focused on designers' opportunities and conditions so that they can work creatively in a financially sustainable way.

Nautilus

Studio Marc Fish

The first version of Nautilus was an experimental coffee table for a coastal home. Inspired by the organic beauty of a half-cut nautilus shell, a new technique was developed to turn 4000 pieces of walnut and sycamore veneer strips into a 10 mm thick logarithmic spiral. For a perfect imitation, a hand-carved fluted pattern was made for the outer part, and Japanese lace paper was used to form the chambers of the shell.

··· Interview with Marc Fish ···

1. What did you take into consideration when it came to the choice of materials and technique?

>>We had no prerequisite for the construction; it is completely unique with no one creating these kinds of shape out of wood. The choice of woods was a direct result of looking for a match to the real shell, in terms of both colours and the eventual texture. We developed a unique material that is made from handmade Japanese paper, which creates the divisions inside the shell.

2. What do you think about biomimetic design?

>>This is fundamental to our design philosophy. We look to nature for all our inspiration and our work looks grown rather than made or constructed. Nature offers such amazing variety: in our lifetime we could not possibly exhaust the opportunities it offers a designer.

3. What is the most unforgettable experience in the design process?

>>Our most unforgettable experience making the first one was putting two weeks' work in the bin. We had to try things and not everything worked for us. This can be quite wasteful in resources and labour costs, but I do feel the results are worth the pain.

Titobowl

Studio photoAlquimia

Designer Carlos Jiménez, Pilar Balsalobre

Titobowl is a vessel specially designed for different dressings like olives with a hollow. Turning the cap of the container upside down transforms it into a toothpick holder. Manufactured with stoneware and olive tree wood, each Titobowl is signed and numbered by hand. The packaging design was inspired by an image of a can of olives. This box is made by hand entirely from cardboard and recycled paper, making it a unique example of eco-packaging.

ESTUDIO MORFOLÓGICO DEL OLIVO

Olivo, Olive, Olivier, Olivier...
- Olea europaea L.
- Fam. oleaceae

Sección transversal

ACEITUNAS

Fruto en drupa

Sección longitudinal

Detalle de hueso o semilla

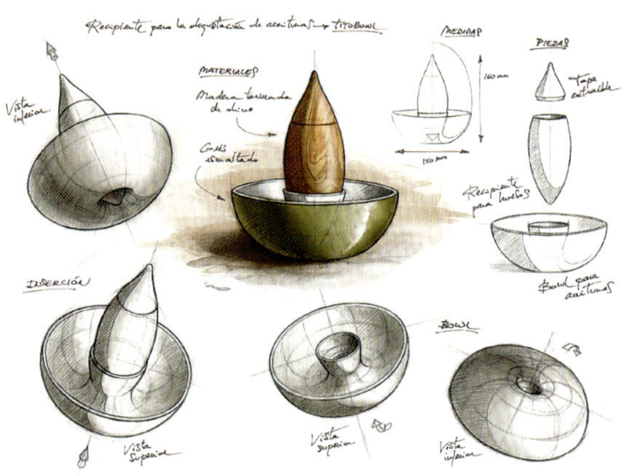

Recipiente para la degustación de aceitunas → TITOBOWL

MATERIALES

Madera torneada de olivo

Gres esmaltado

MEDIDAS

160 mm

150 mm

PIEZAS

Tapa extraíble

Recipiente para huesos

Bowl para aceitunas

Vista inferior

INSERCIÓN

Vista superior

Vista superior

BOWL

Vista inferior

ESTUDIO DE FUNCIONALIDAD DE TITOBOWL

Acabado: Aceite de lino 100% natural y pulido

Tacto cálido y suave

Los huesos quedan ocultos a la vista

Estudio de color

OK

OK

Uso de la tapa como palillero para aceitunas sin hueso y otros aperitivos

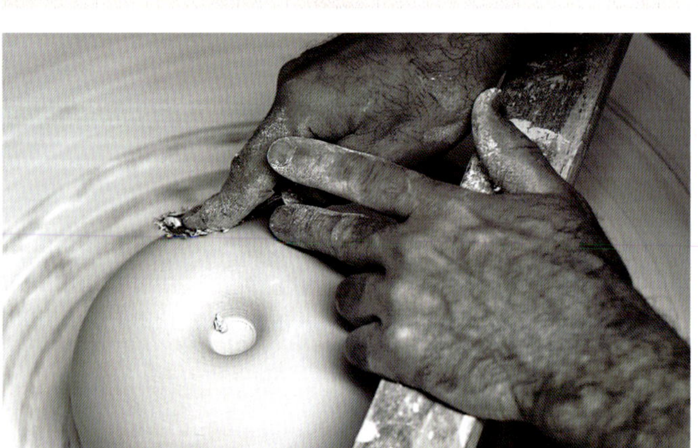

Form

titobowl
NATURA IMITATIS
by photoAlquimia

Goat Mug

Studio Desnahemisfera

Designer Damir Islamović, Klemen Smrtnik, Dejan Kos

This coffee mug was designed to encourage the use of sustainable drinking cups, supporting the client's views on environmental protection. The distinctive horn shape alludes to the legend of the discovery of coffee. The mug comes with two types of strap, allowing customers to carry their drinks with ease and style. The removable leather holder also works as a mug stand.

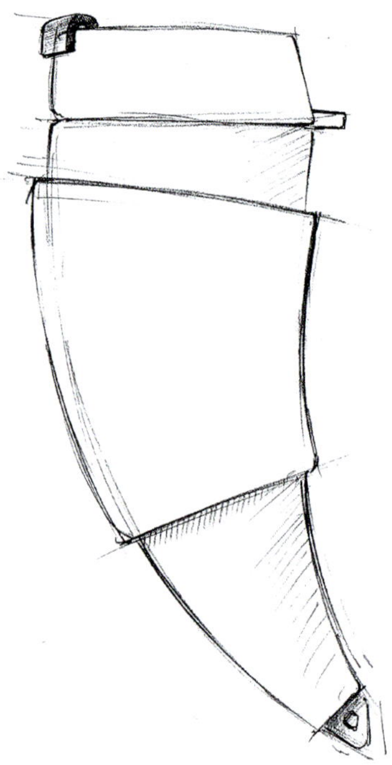

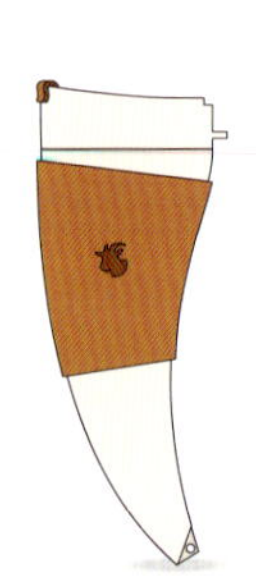

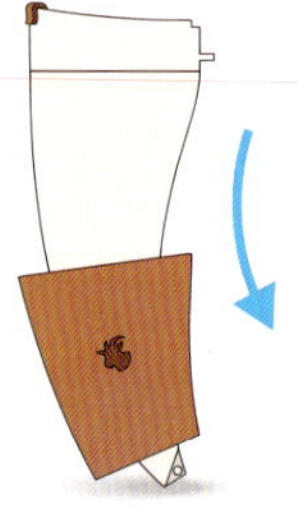

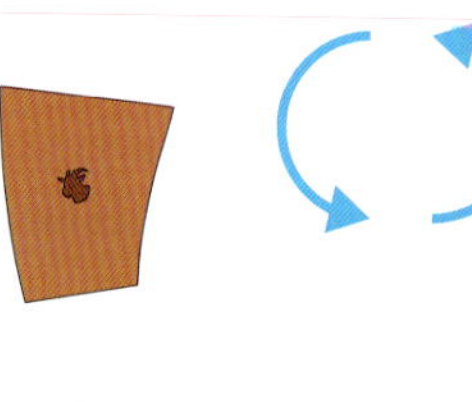

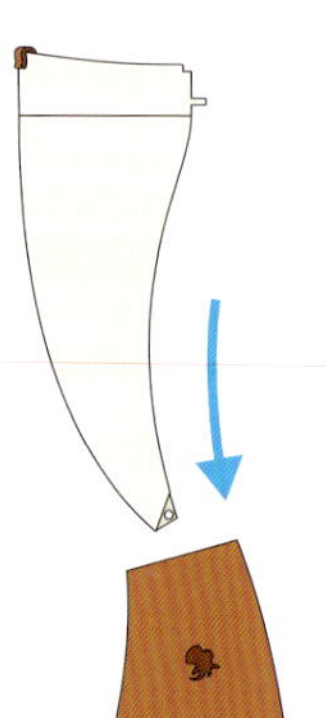

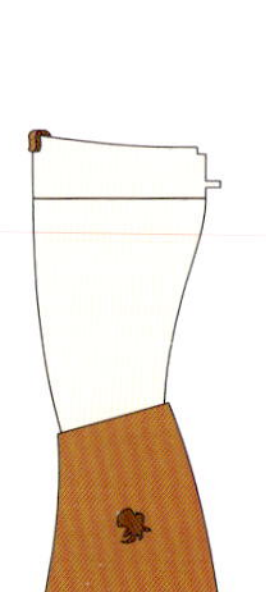

Ajorí

Studio photoAlquimia

Designer Carlos Jimenez, Pilar Balsalobre

Ajorí is a creative solution to organizing and storing culinary condiments, inspired by the elegant form of the bulb of garlic. This kitchen accessory holds six containers, each designed for the seasoning of several dishes, and adapted to the culinary customs of different countries. Created only with natural materials and using a mixture of industrial and artisanal processes, Ajorí is an eco-friendly product. The packaging imitates the skin of garlic and only natural and biodegradable materials are used in its manufacture.

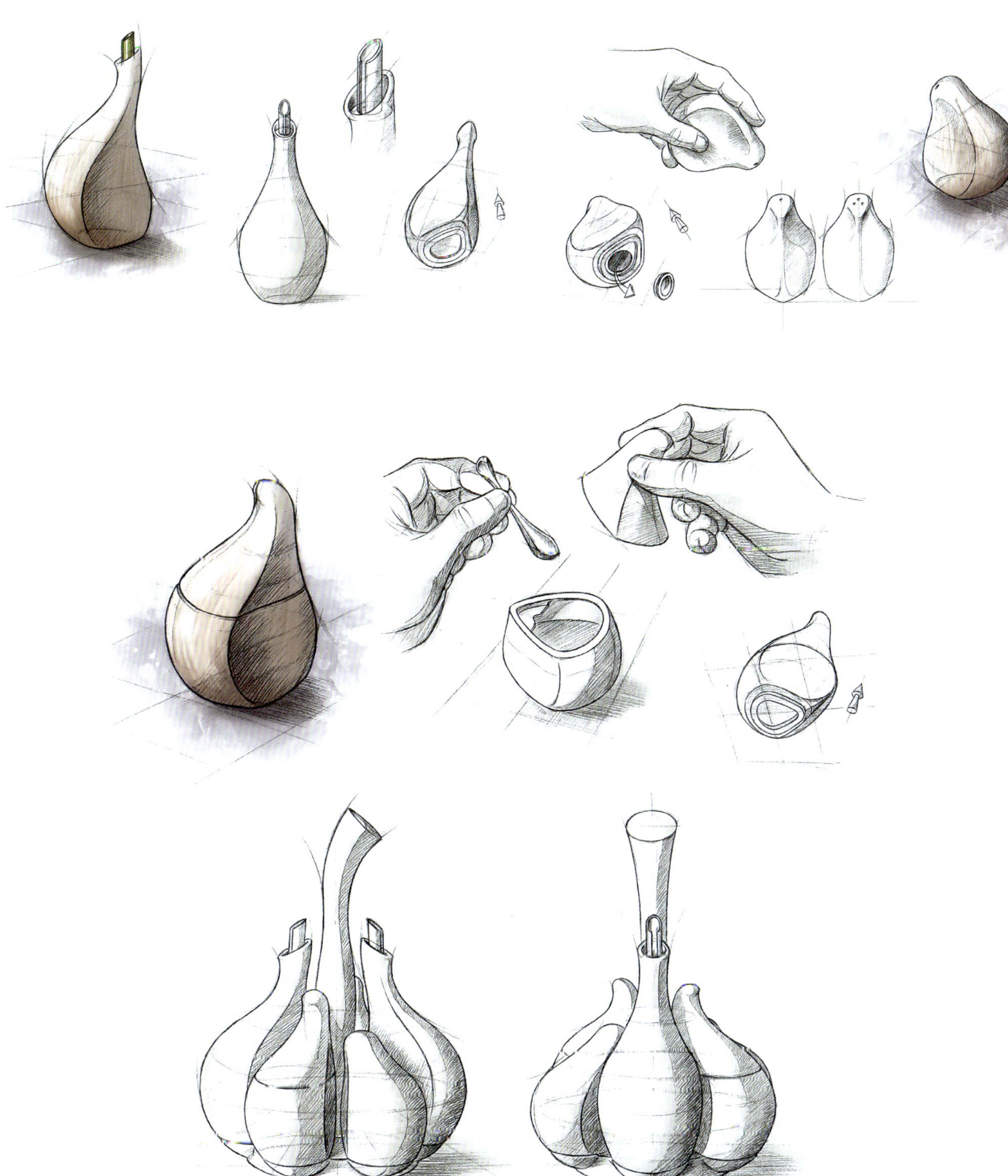

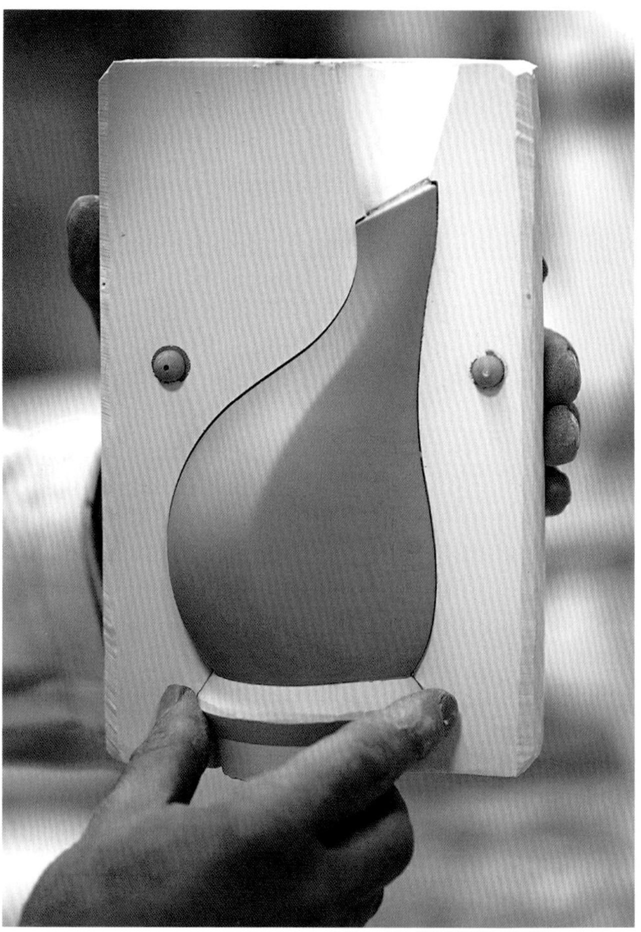

Lotus Waterproof Speaker

Designer Lim Loren

While listening to the music, the user can also feel its rhythm through the movement of water: Lotus uses vibration to create waves that correspond to the music's beat. It is designed to be placed on any surface and is able to float on water. The intensity of the waves created is based on the frequency of the music. This waterproof speaker aims to increase the interaction between the product and the user.

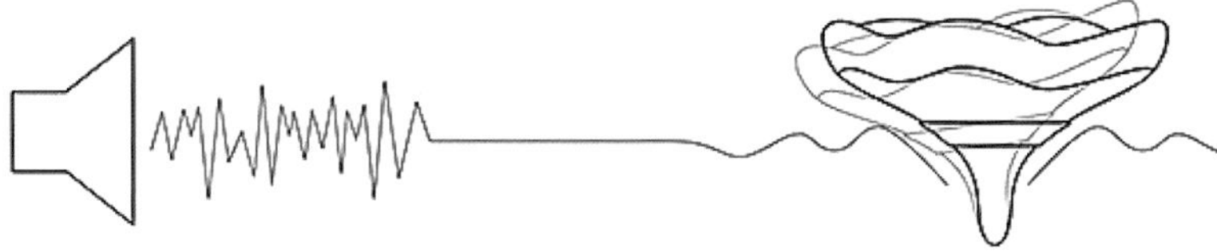

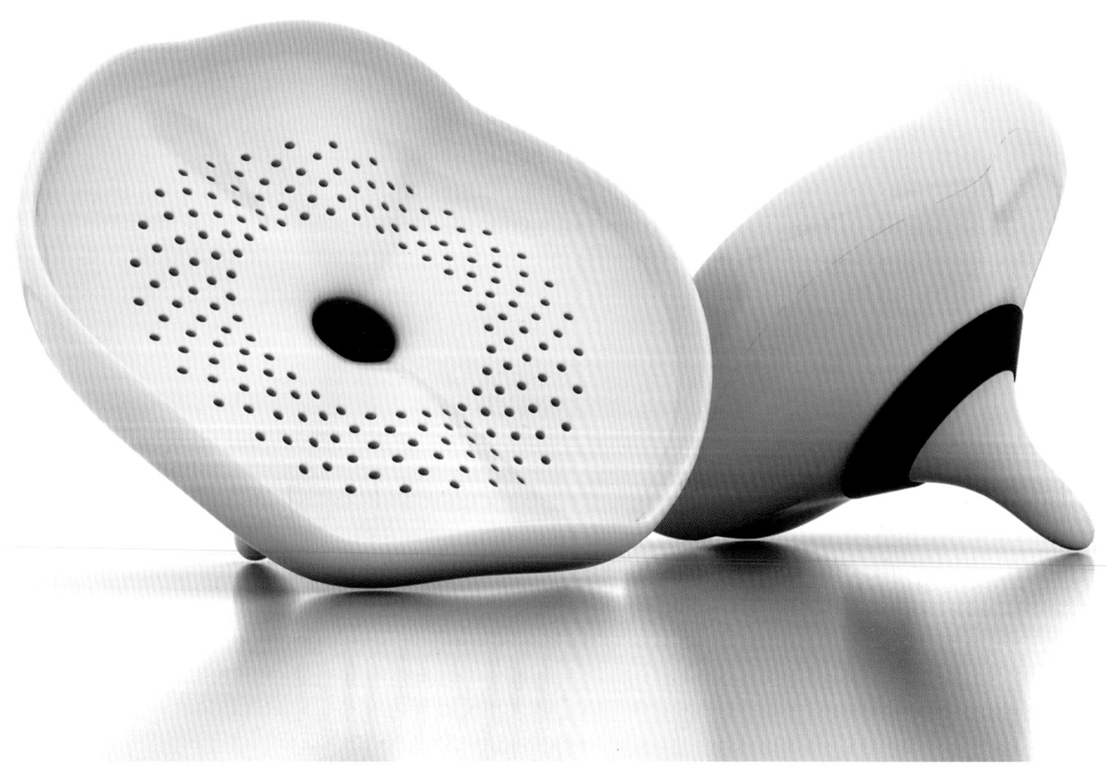

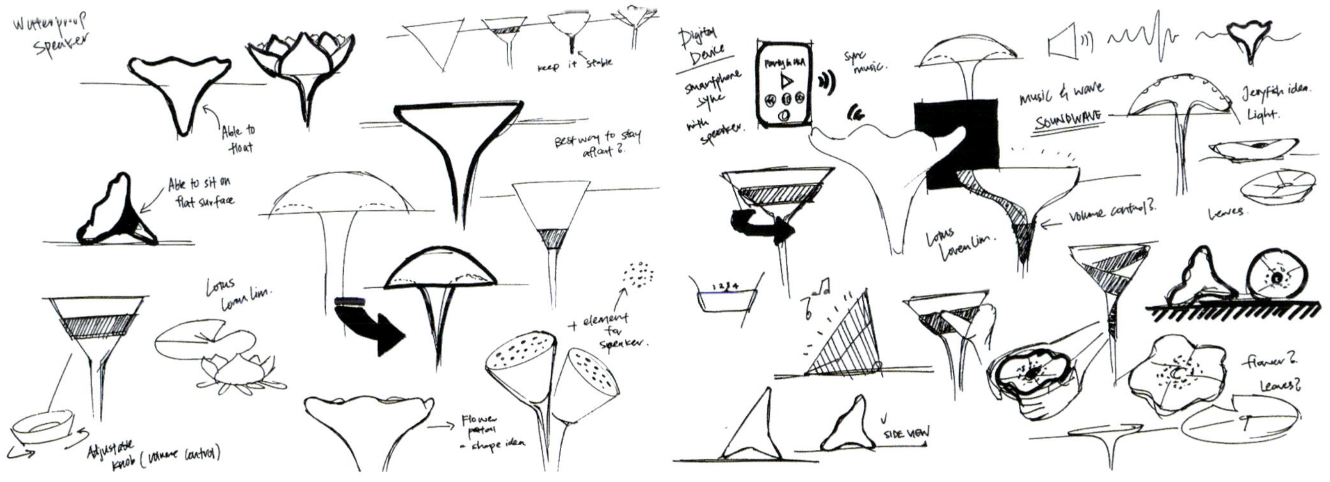

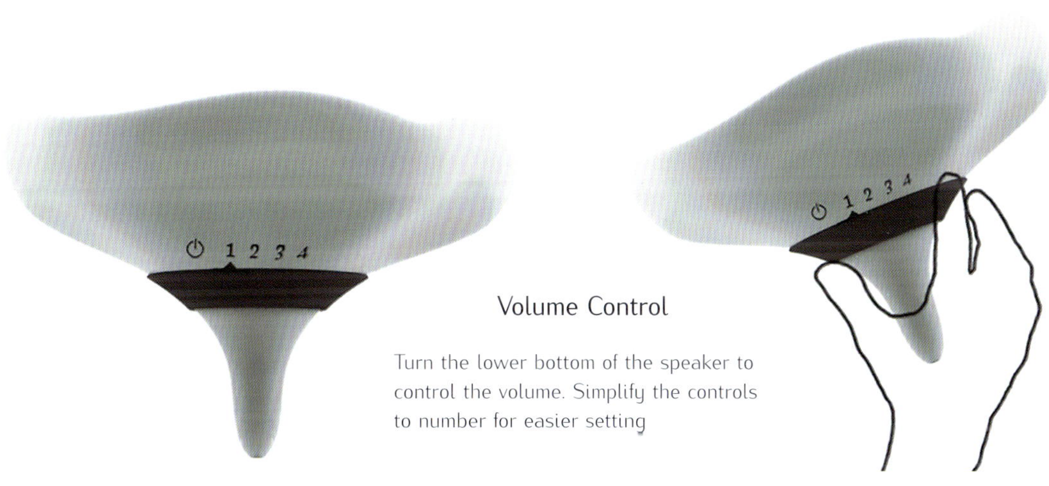

Volume Control

Turn the lower bottom of the speaker to control the volume. Simplify the controls to number for easier setting

Technology Used

Vibrating Disk Motor

Waterproof Speakers

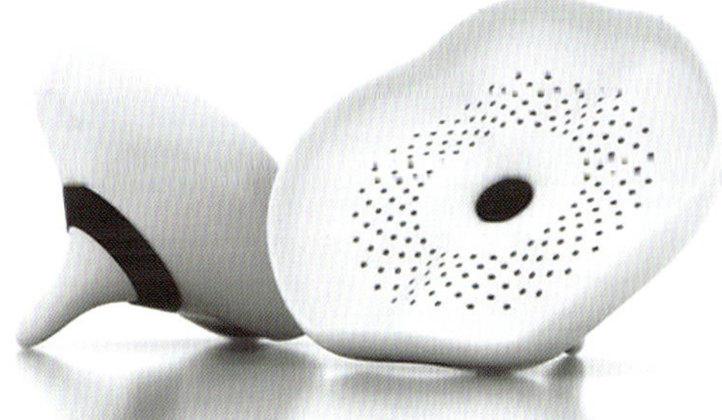

Nautilus Light

Designer Rebecca Asquith

Inspired by a nautilus shell, this kit-set hanging lampshade rolls back into itself to mimic the shell's complex organic form. When switched on, the light filters through the layers of timber to give a warm glow and patterns the space beautifully. The work is made of European beech plywood and stainless steel spider, nuts and plastic rivets. The parts were nested tightly together during the cutting process to minimize material waste.

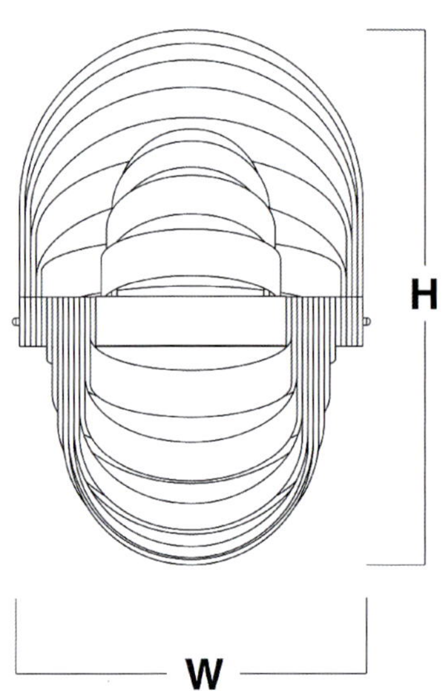

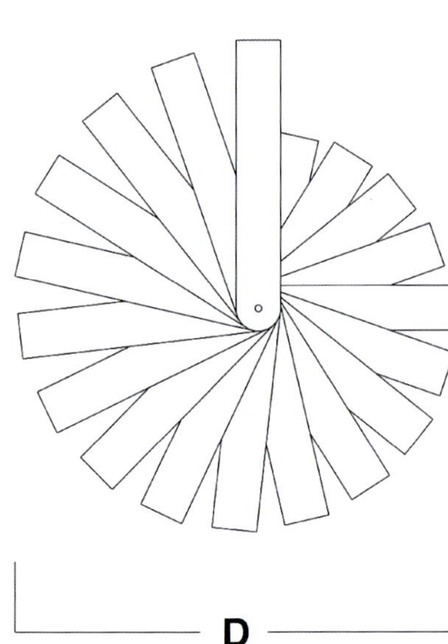

Small: **H** 420mm, **W** 325mm, **D** 370mm
Medium: **H** 505mm, **W** 375mm, **D** 440mm

Fresh LED Desk Lamp

Designer Victor Vetterlein

Five tendrils designed to look like thick stalks of green grass serve as the bendable fingers of the light. They may be pointed and directed in different directions as needed. The lamp is composed of a rubber-coated metal base, neoprene-coated solid aluminum arms and dimmable LED lights with acrylic magnifying lenses.

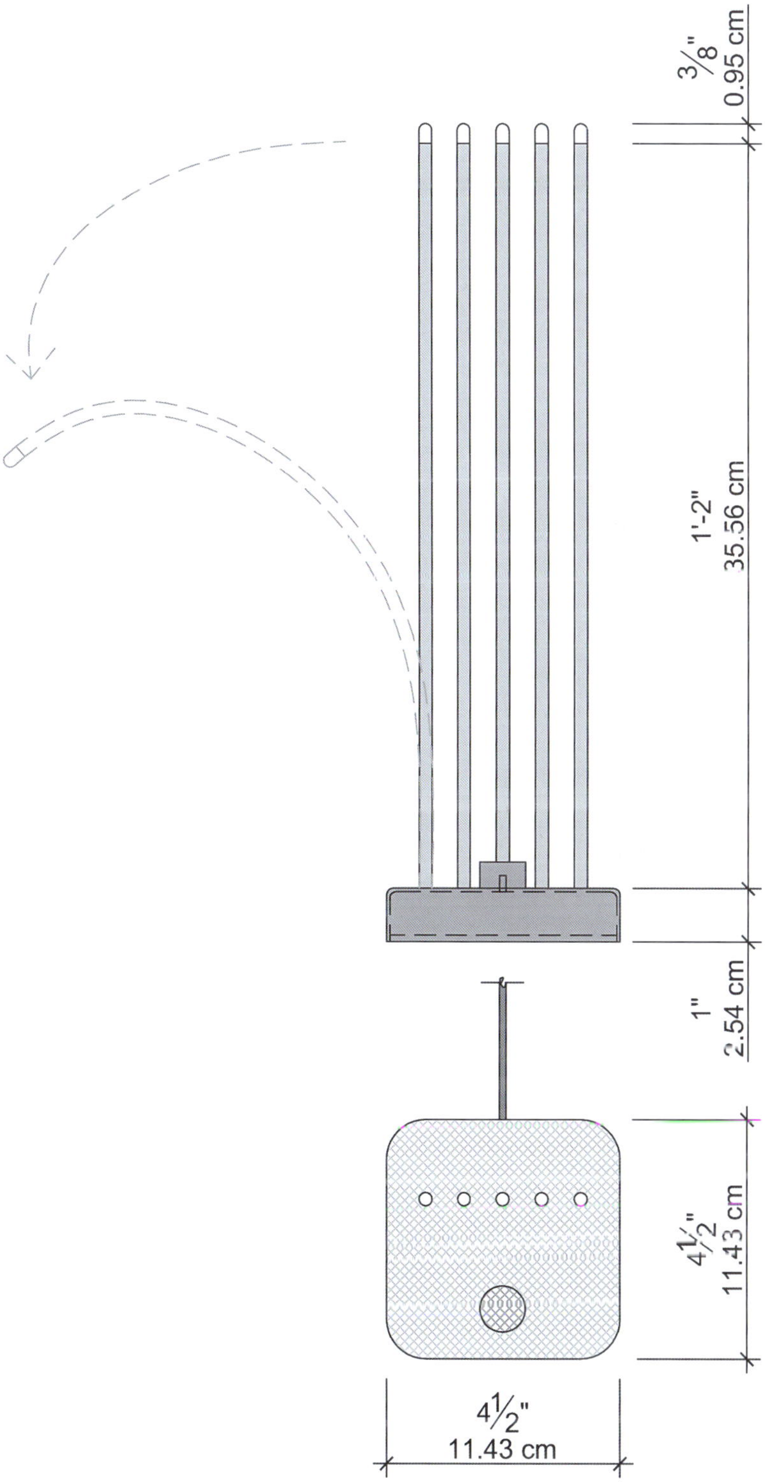

3⁄8"
0.95 cm

1'-2"
35.56 cm

1"
2.54 cm

4½"
11.43 cm

4½"
11.43 cm

Crick

Designer Pedro Feduchi

This stool pays tribute to the researchers who discovered the geometrical law and inner order of DNA. The project started with "Photo 51", the famous X-ray diffraction image of DNA, as its only visual clue. The implicit functional structural order found in the photo was the inspiration for the inverse process of design. The chairs are stackable for easy storage and to save space.

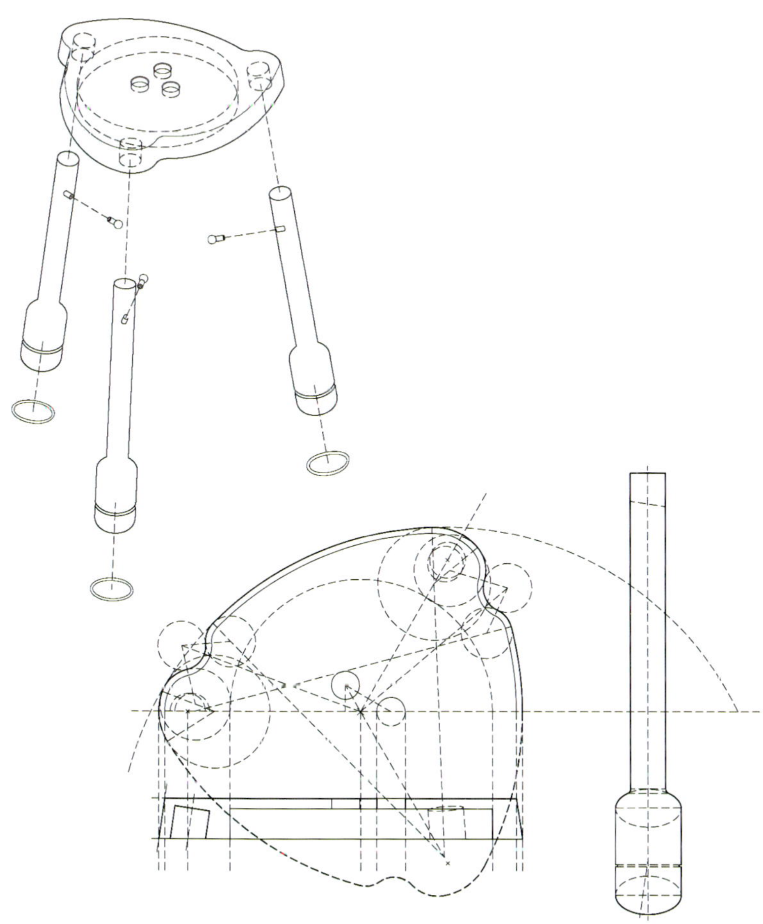

Humus

Studio Paradisiartificiali

This collection is dedicated to express gratitude to Mother Nature and her infinite generosity, with its vascular design encouraging the preservation of the roots of flowers.

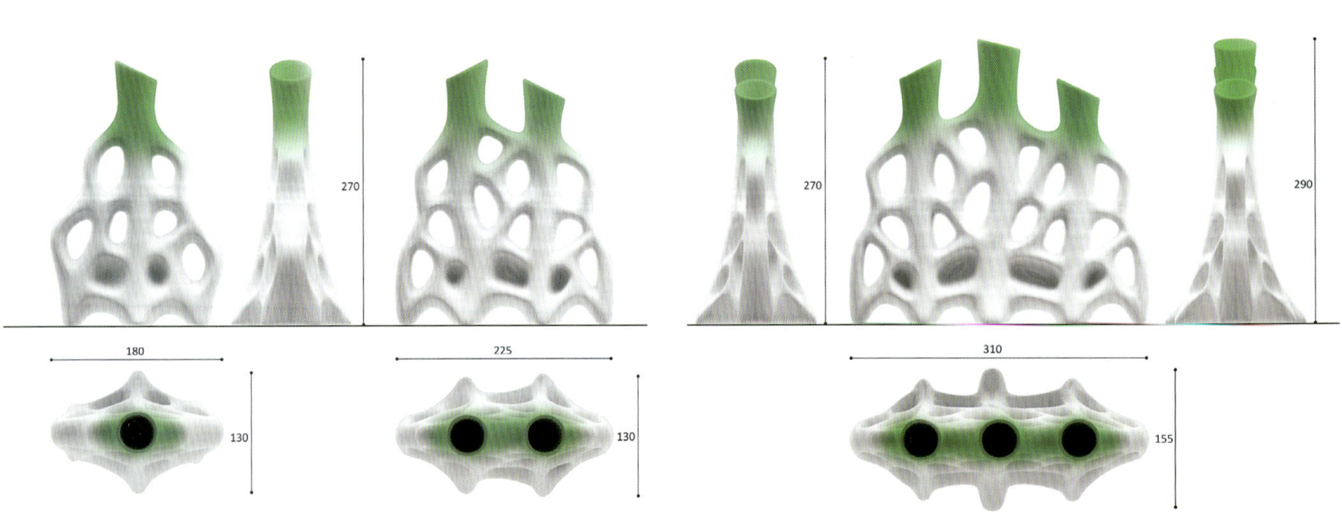

In vascular plants, the root is the organ of a plant that typically lies below the surface of the soil. However, roots can also be aerial.

Abramo please do not cut life!

the project of a vase as a symbolic act to ask forgiveness for having committed a cruel act.

"... dai diamanti non nasce niente, dal letame nascono i fiori"

F. De Andre's song

What hold flowers? Roots
What feeds flowers? Roots
Why did you cut the flower?

Every flower
has its root,
every root
has its vase.

How much water does a flower need?
The water that can be held by its roots.

1 stem 2 stems 3 stems

CAPILLARY VASE
or else
COLLECTION of FERTILE VASES

Honeycomb Lamp

Designer Margaret Barry

This spherical lamp of hexagonal cells is an investigation of geometry and illusion. A slight angular warp allows the cells to nest in a curved surface in clustered fragments that, when arranged strategically, suggest a complete sphere, making a geometrically impossible configuration seem completely credible. The mahogany ply walls of the extruded cells propel light outwards, while gaps in the outer shell evoke curiosity about the interior. By adjusting the dimmer switch, the user can experience a wide range of visual qualities.

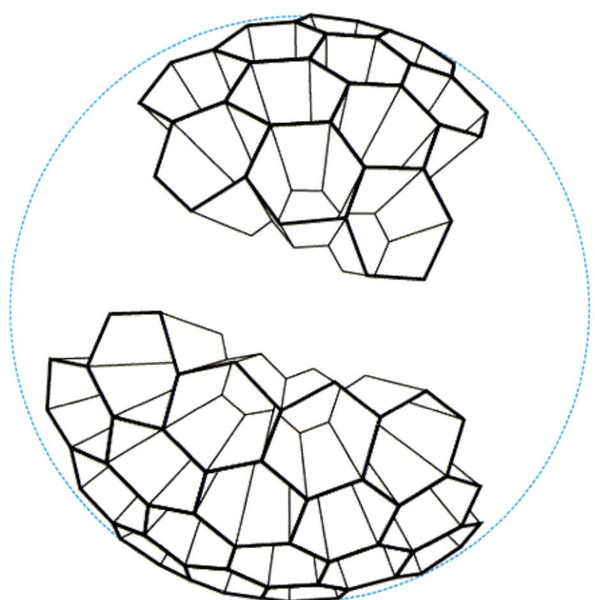

Le Mobilier de Compagnie

Studio ibride

Designer Benoit Convers

The brief was to enhance the affection between the consumers and their furniture, striking a balance between nature and art, techniques and emotions. The collection includes 12 different pieces of furniture, such as JOE the bear bookshelf, DIVA the ostrich console and JUNON the illuminated goose.

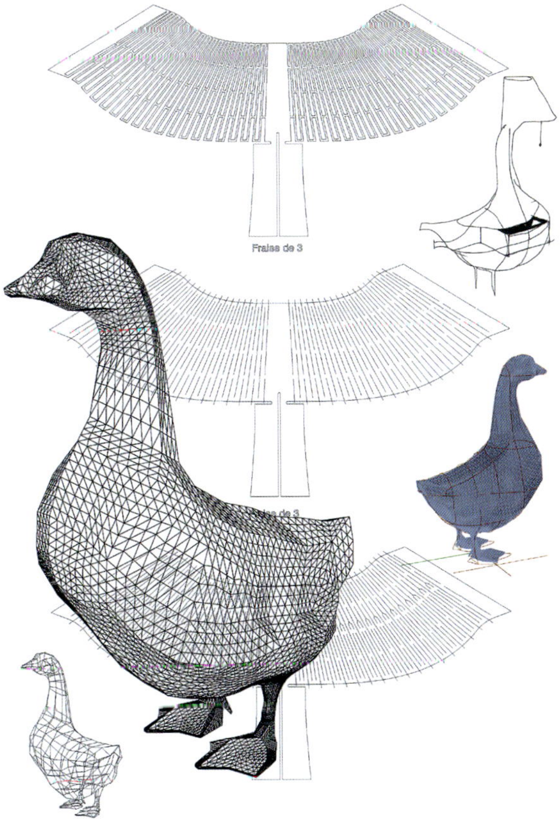

Fraisa de 3

The Heart

Studio Kosmos Project

Designer Ewa Bochen, Maciej Jelski

The Heart is a wine decanter in the shape of a human heart, offering comment on the contemporary human spiritual condition. Every piece is uniquely handmade from borosilicate glass by the glass craft master.

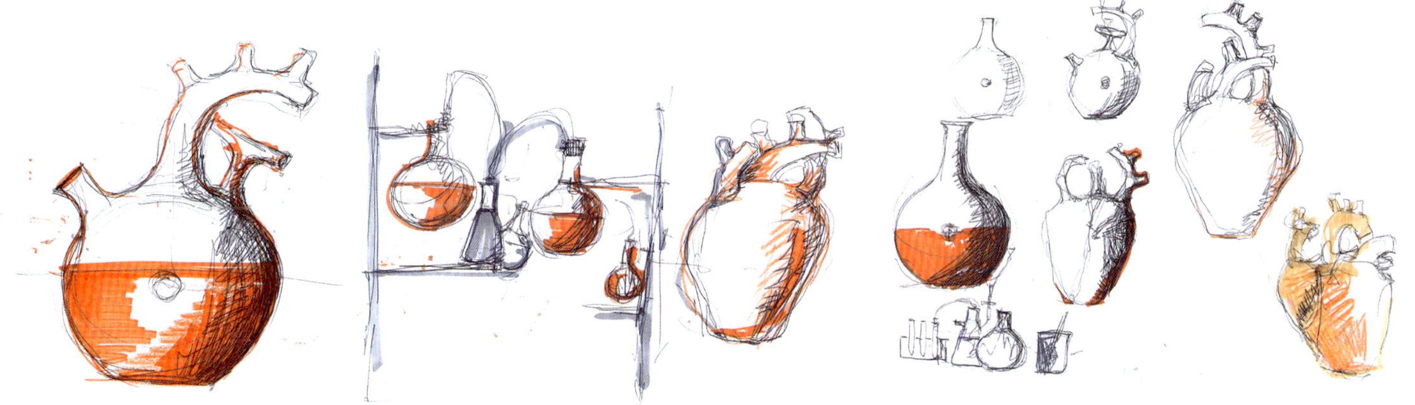

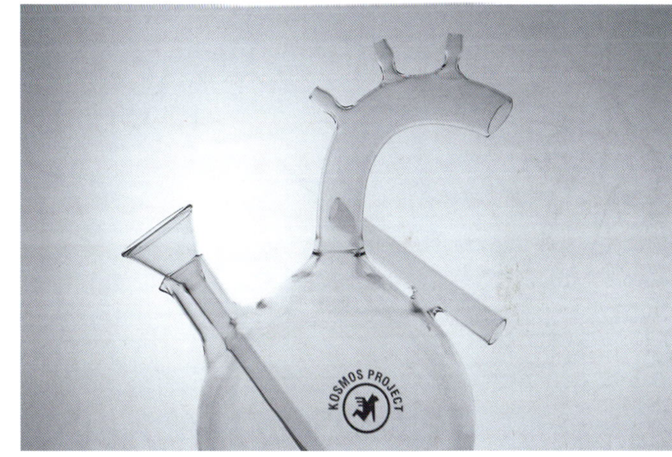
KOSMOS PROJECT

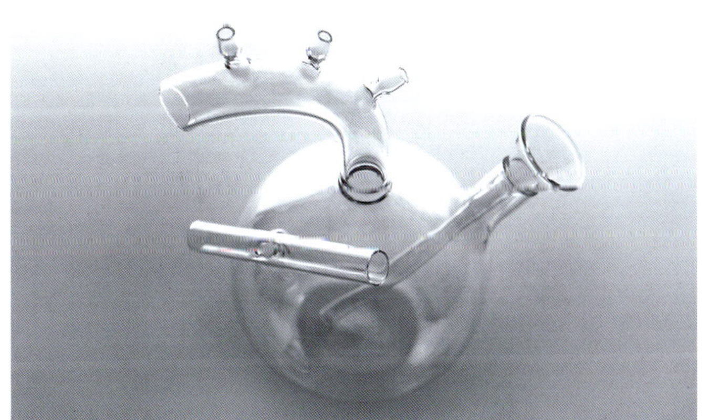

Skull Chair

Studio Chic Sin Design

An obsession with the structure of the human body and the expressive motif of skull has led to the creation of this huge skull, with the upper part of the movable jaw as the backrest of the chair. The surface is knitted with five different-colored yarns, making the shape and the hues as similar as possible to those of a real skull. The likeness stands in stark contrast with the irrational size of the chair, delivering an especially strong visual impact.

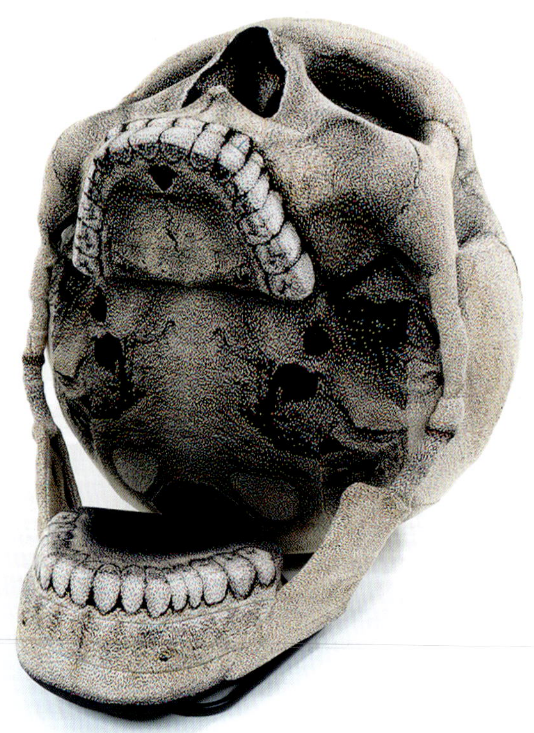

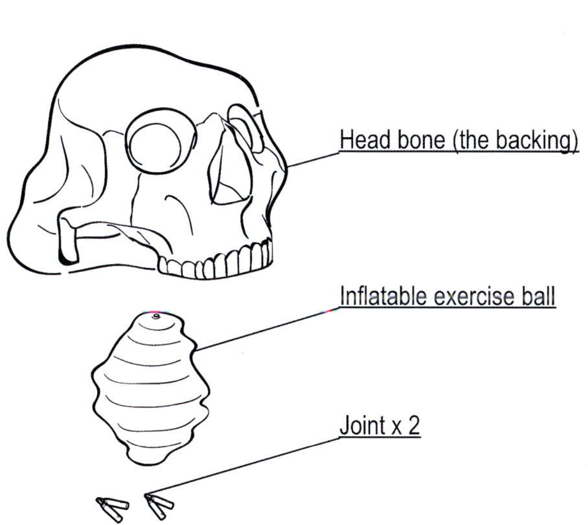
Head bone (the backing)
Inflatable exercise ball
Joint x 2

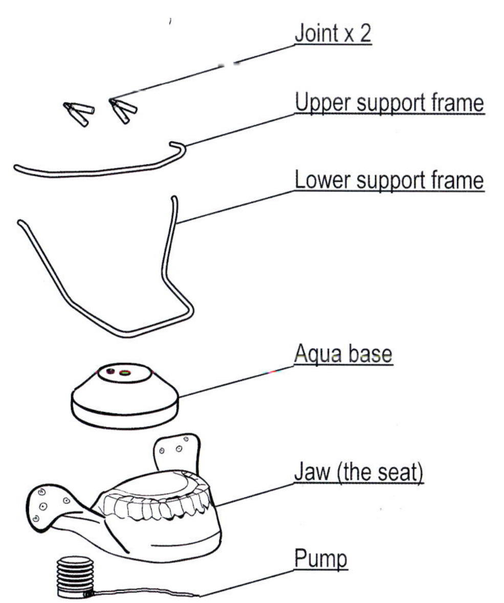
Joint x 2
Upper support frame
Lower support frame
Aqua base
Jaw (the seat)
Pump

Baum

Designer Davide Macullo

Baum is a chair made of 144 core blocks of solid pear wood treated with natural wax and assembled using hidden elements of made-to-measure stainless steel screws. The design began with a freehand sketch of a tree, a spontaneous stroke of the pencil. It produced a structure that is reminiscent of a ginkgo leaf, conveying the pleasure of an intimate relationship with nature.

BINKO → BAUM

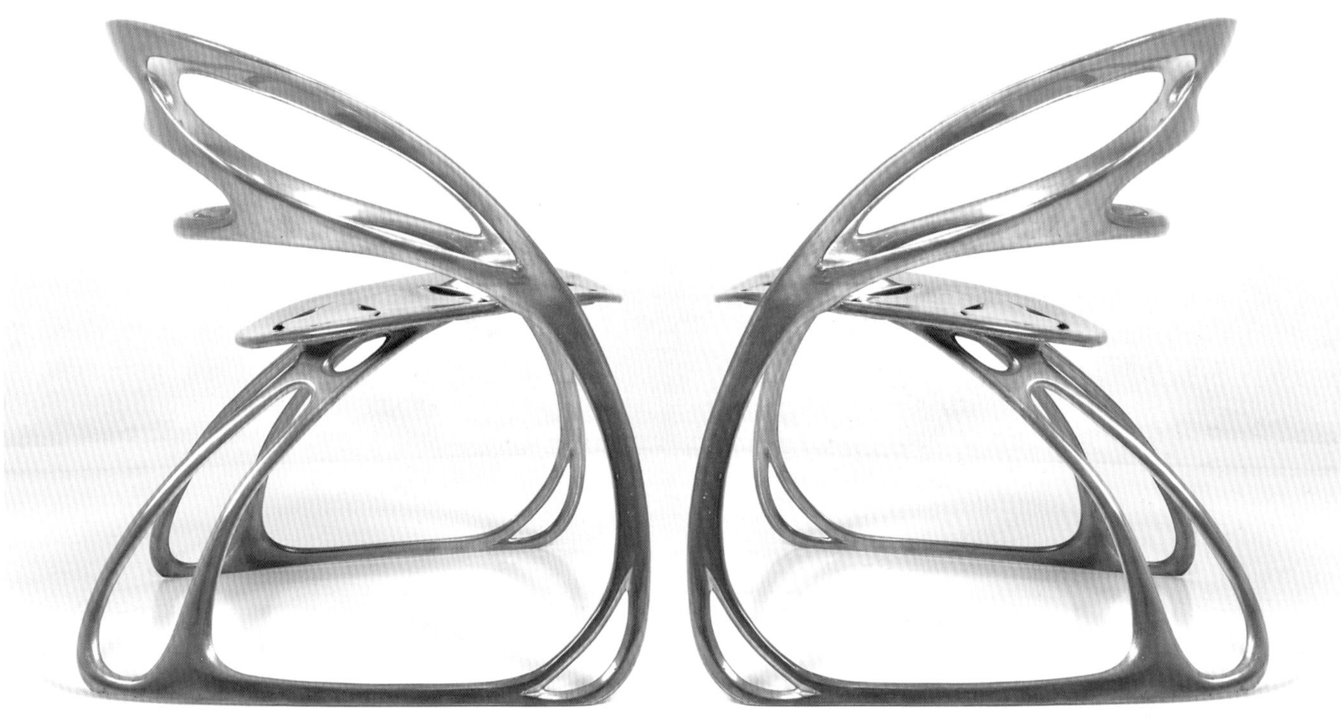

Butterfly Chairs

Designer Santo & Jean Ya

The design aims to maximize the visual power of the schematics of the wings of the monarch butterfly aesthetically and structurally. This piece is part of a collection that explores various metalworking techniques. The studio uses aluminum alloy and the lost wax casting technique to produce lightness and durability, as well as the possibility of playing with organic shapes.

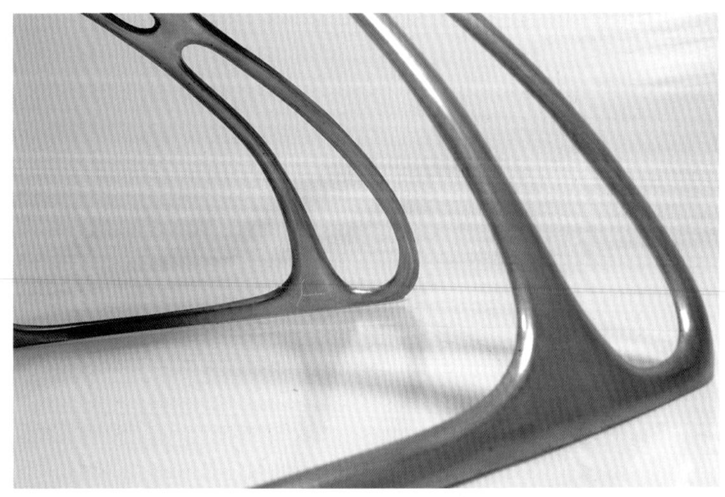

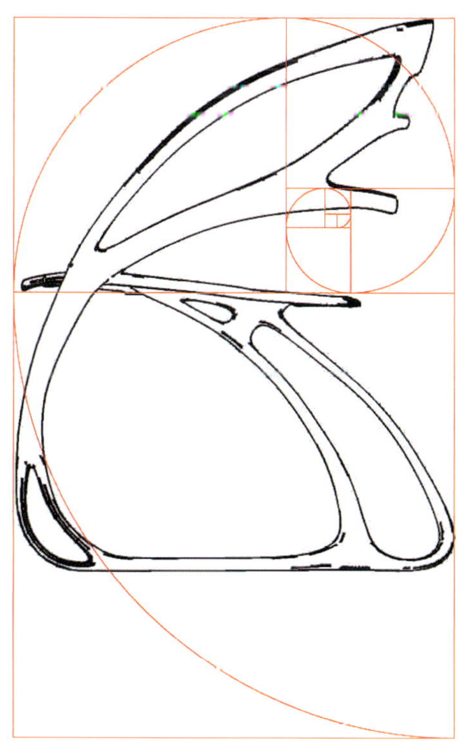

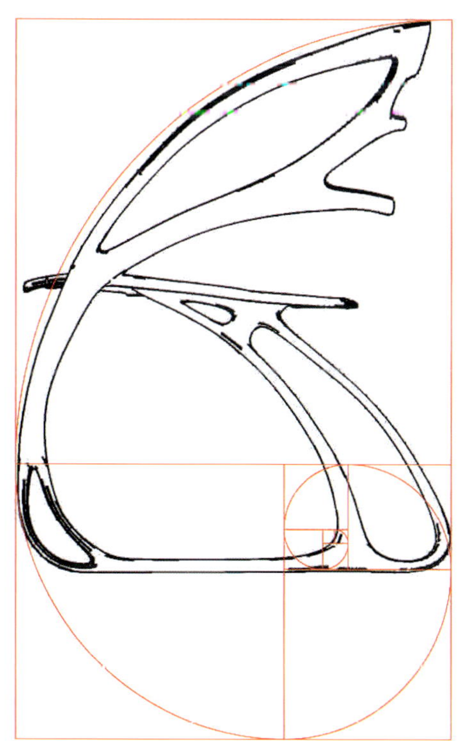

Skell

Designer Mery von Bernard, Valentina Villa-Gómez

To celebrate the 100th anniversary of the renowned Danish designer Hans J. Wegner, the designers created a chair in honor of his legacy—Shell, one of his most representative chairs. The designers modernized the design by using iron bars to form the skeleton of the new chair, and maintained the use of curved plywood, which was the essence of the original version. The finishing processes like the electrostatic dust paint for the structure and the eco-friendly pigmentation of the wood allow for customized combinations.

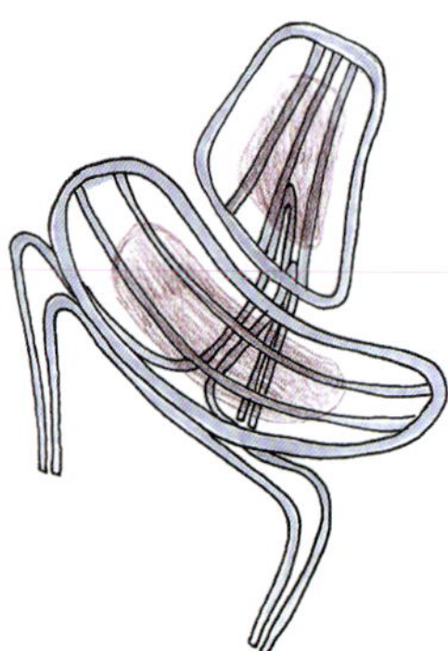

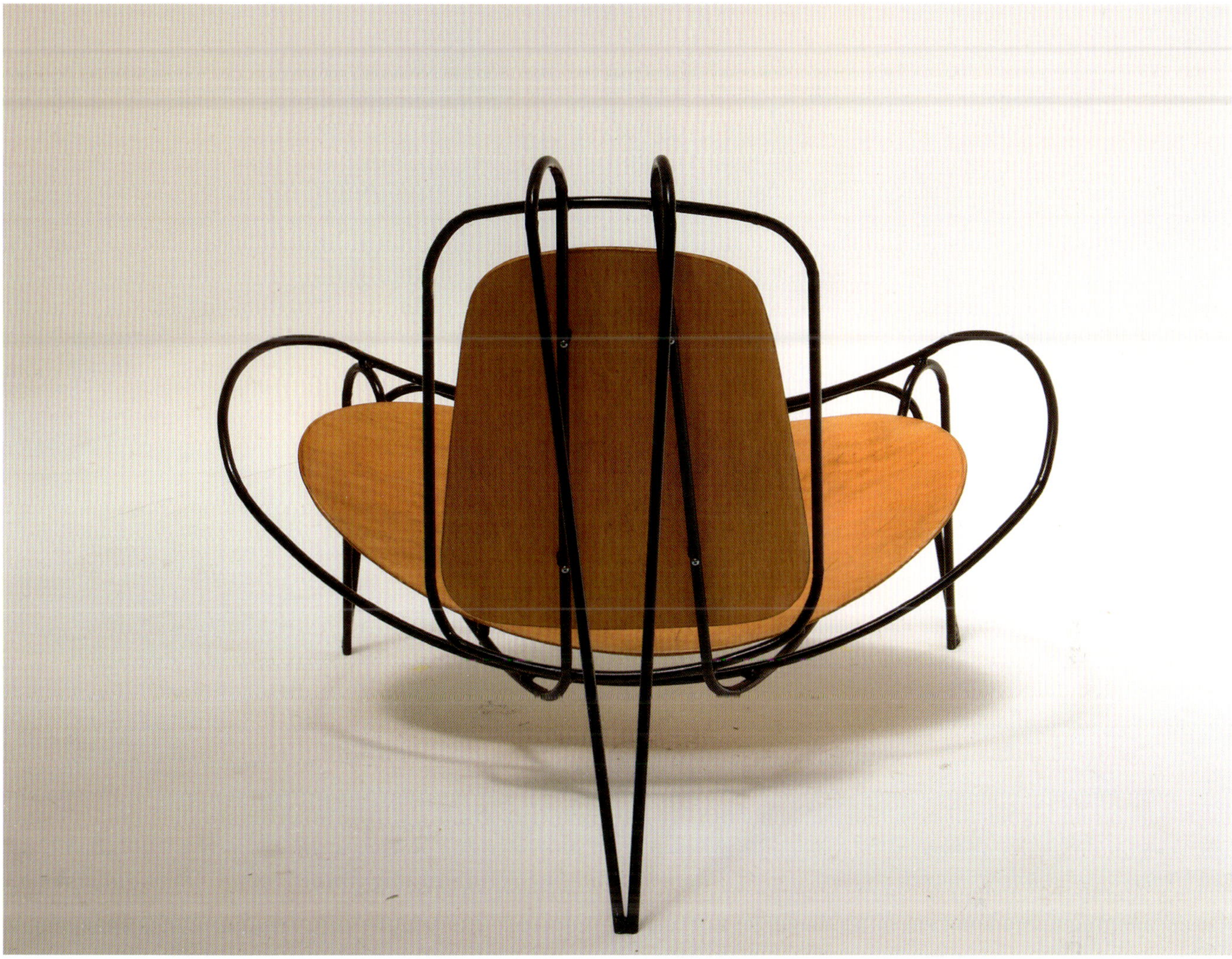

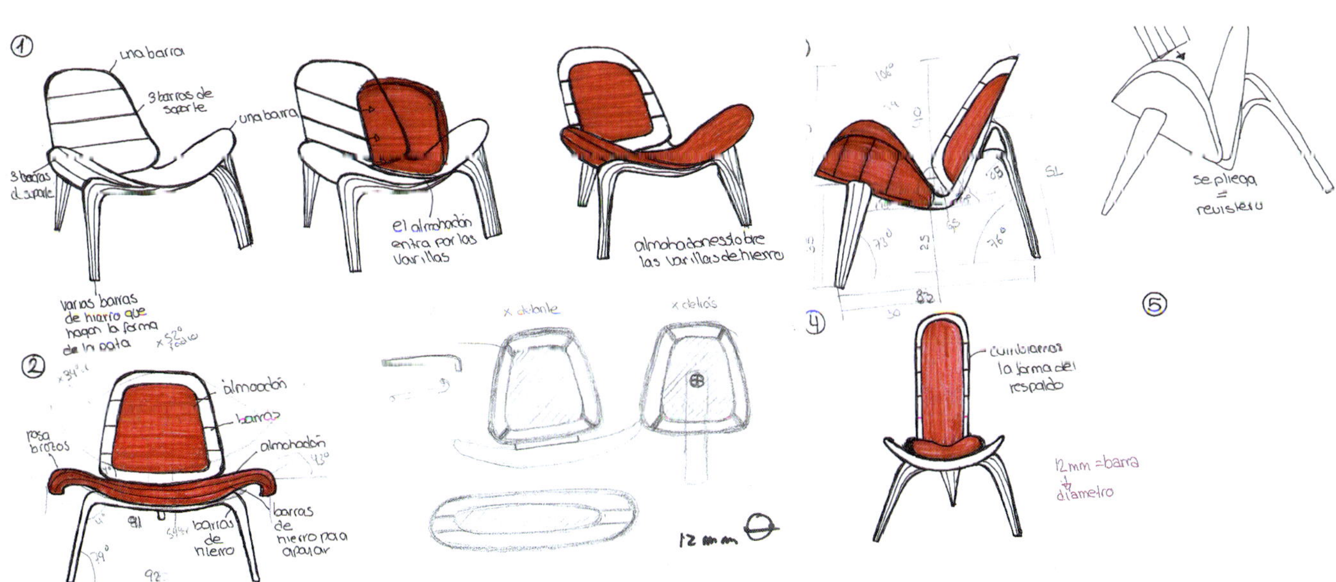
una barra
3 barras de soporte
una barra
3 barras d. soporte
varias barras de hierro que hagan la forma de la pata
el almohadón entra por las varillas
almohadones sobre las varillas de hierro
x delante
x detrás
almoadón
barras
posa brazos
almohadón
barras de hierro
barras de hierro para apoyar
12 mm
se pliega = revistero
la forma del respaldo
12 mm = barra diametro

Cactus Lamp

Designer Luca Pupulin

This project was born from the idea of exploiting the complexity of plant shapes using sintered polyamide, an innovative material, and the 3D printing process. The succulent plant Opuntia ficus indica was the inspiration for the Cactus Lamp because of its bilateral morphology, where the two parts fit together perpendicularly. The lamp can be turned from a desk lamp into two separate spotlights, and is suitable for either a domestic or public context. The bulbs can be supplied with either electric or induced current (the removable part).

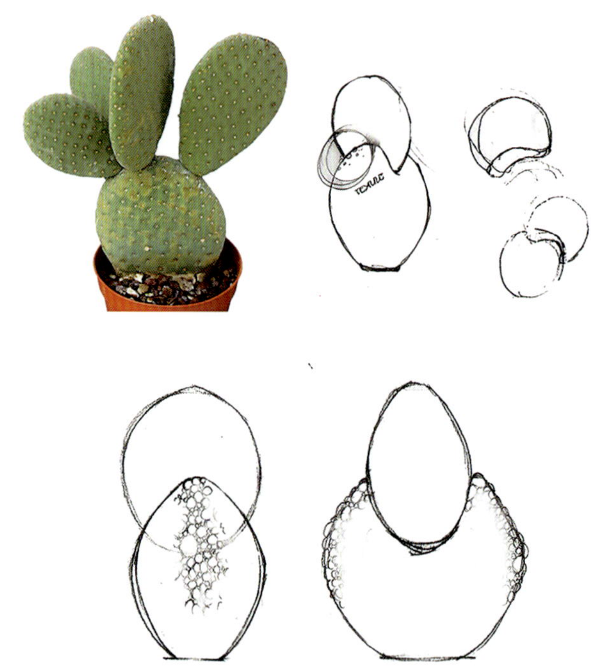

Form

Loosers

Designer Francesca Barchiesi

The Loosers cups are the result of a visual reinterpretation of the octopus into simple and joyful ceramic mugs that are also funny and colorful characters. Realized by slip casting the porcelain into a four-part plaster mold, the cups are thick and resistant with a glossy finish. The casting holes are hidden at the bottom of the cup's feet, while the eyes are painted by hand.

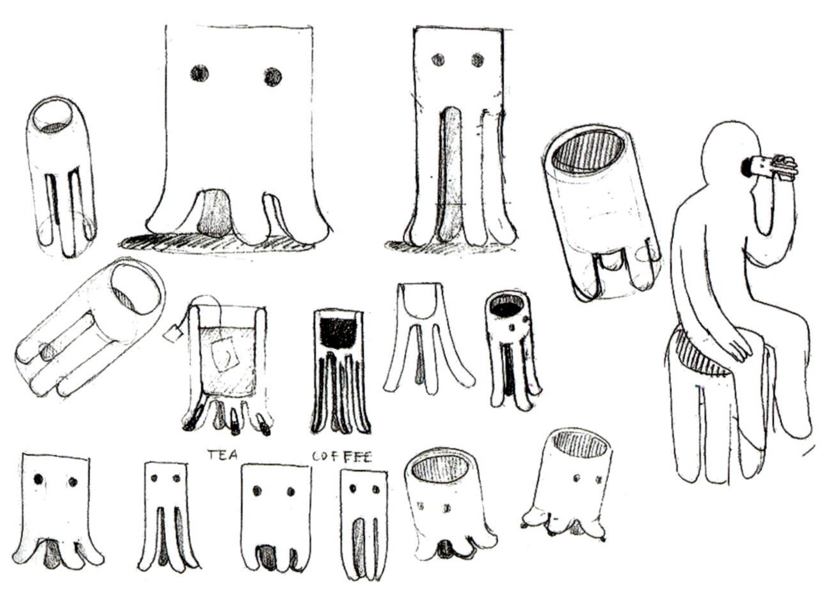

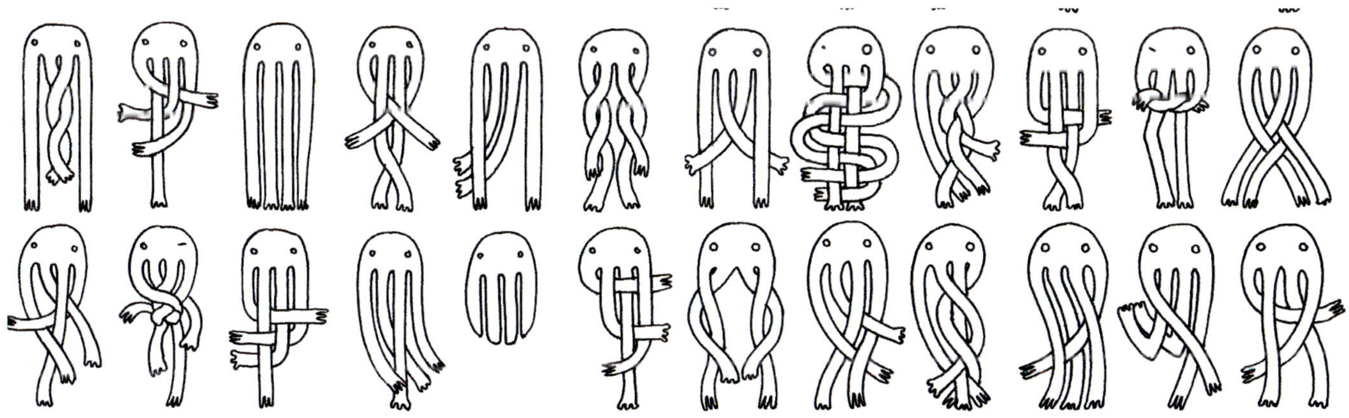

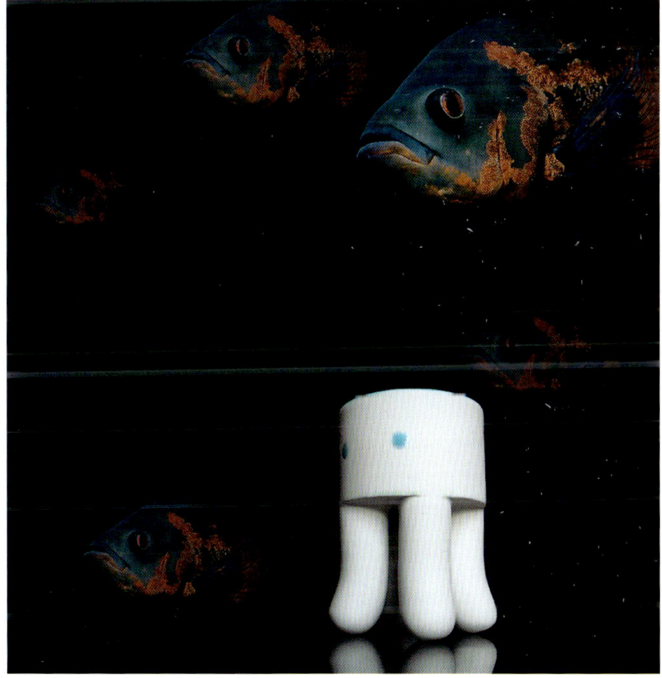

ADAPT

Designer Christian Sjöström

The intention of the designer was to create a floor lamp for indoor use with a design that easily could be changed and transformed. With inspiration from the worm's ability to freely move its body in any direction, ADAPT was created. ADAPT fulfills its function as a lamp but at the same time it's perceived as a decorative object, putting the material in focus. This balance between function, form and material is what makes it interesting and different: it is a lamp that crawls.

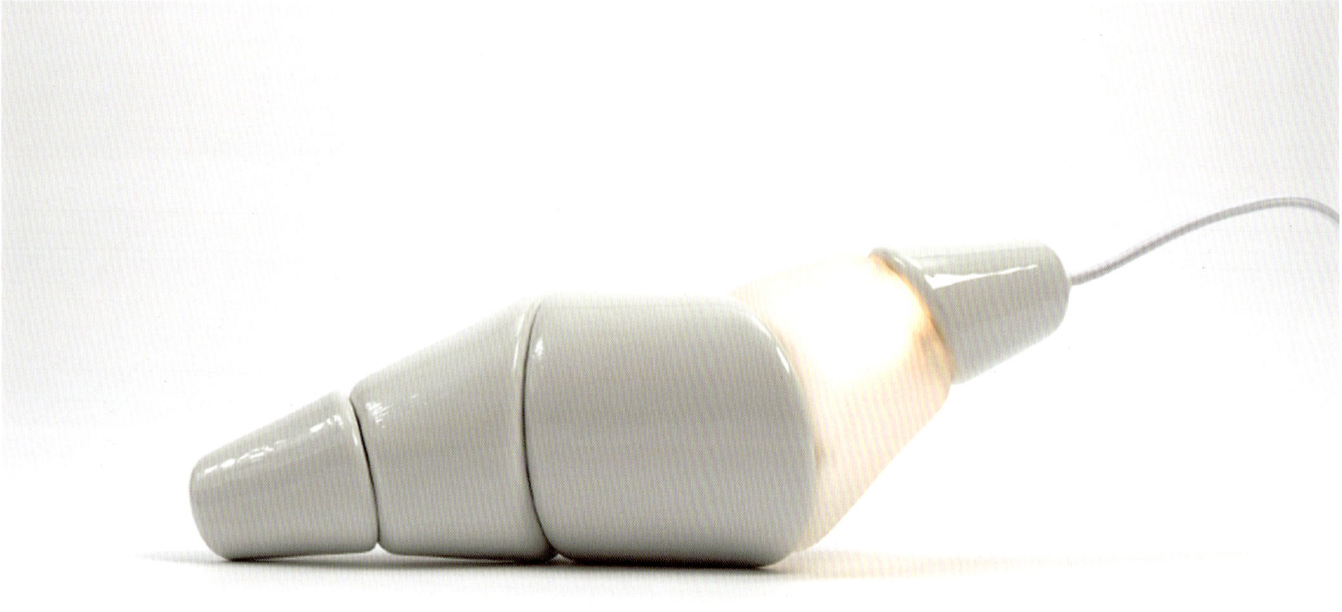

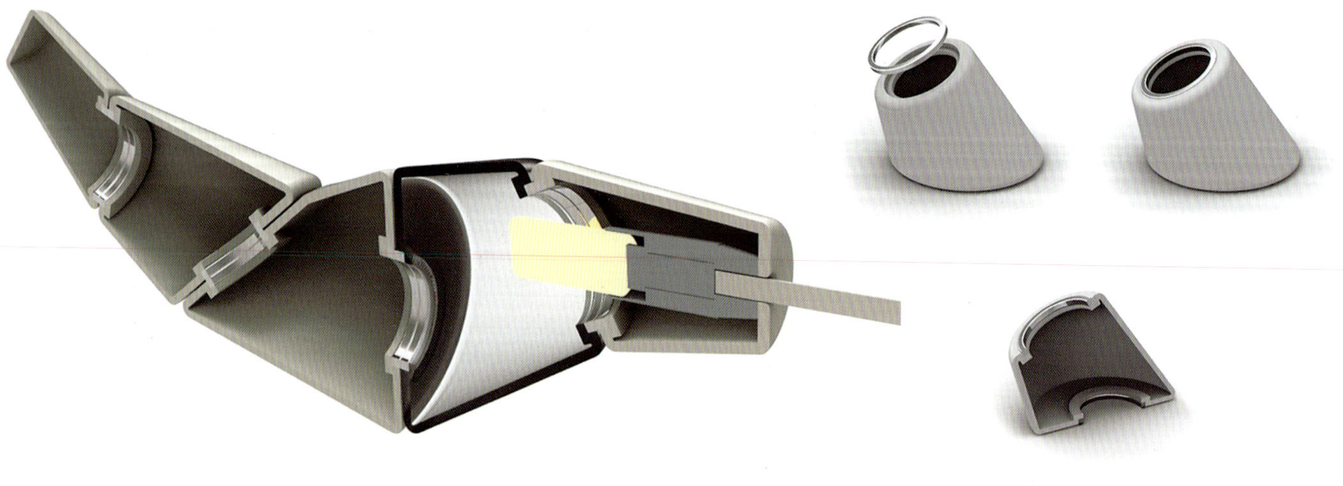

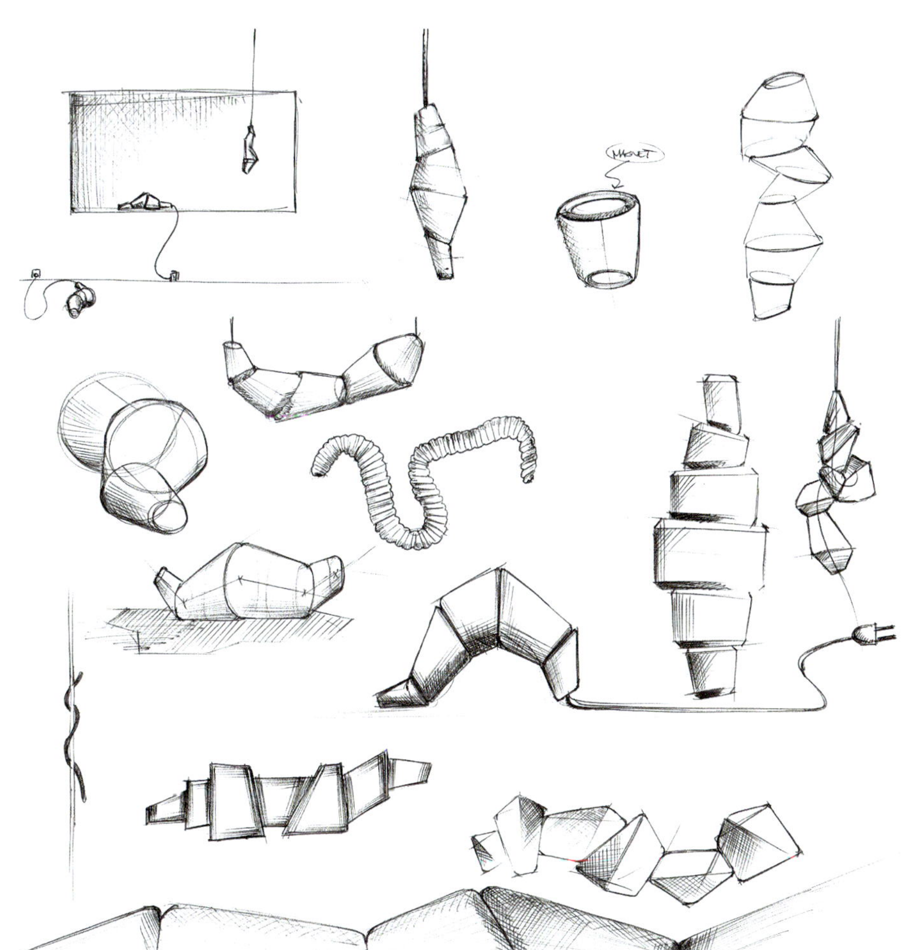
MAGNET

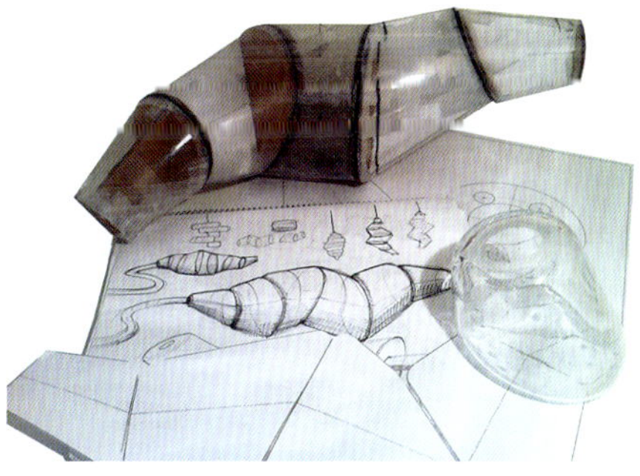

Vanessa

Studio Bonaldo S.p.A.

Designer Bartoli Design

Made of multi-laminar walnut-painted wood, Vanessa is a fixed table characterized by a glass table top, available in different shapes and sizes, and legs that are in an evocative butterfly shape.

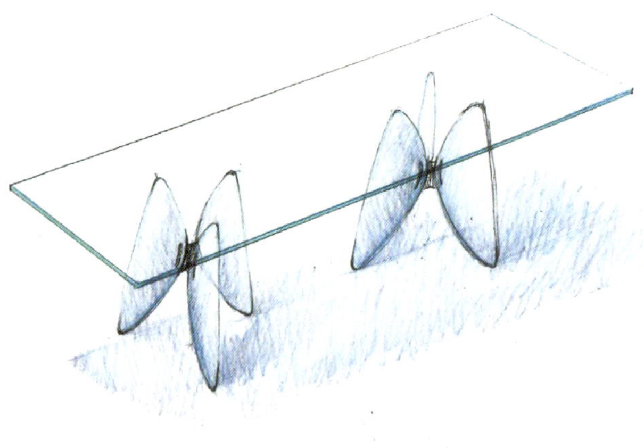

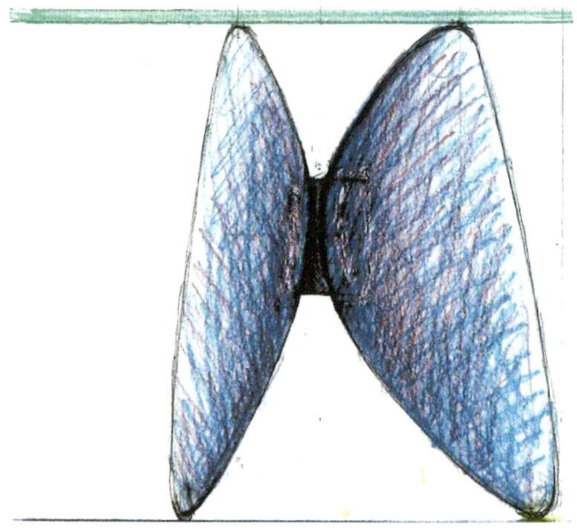

Daisy Chair

Designer Dominika Drezner

This foldable chair is especially designed for children so they can sit as they prefer on the floor or in a chair. The transformation from a daisy flower seat to a drum-like stool is inspiring and entertaining for children. Being space saving and easy to carry, it is an ideal amenity for school.

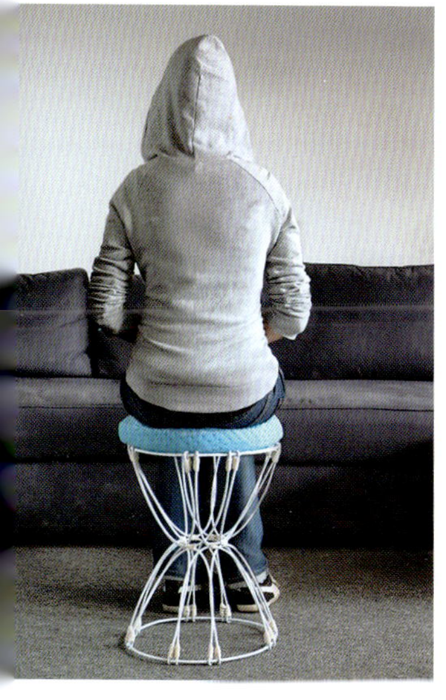

Sending Animals

Designer Marcantonio Raimondi Malerba

The designer aimed to investigate the relationship between man and nature through a synthesis of art and design inspired by animal shapes. The farm animals were turned into life-sized cabinets, which are produced using the same manufacturing process as wooden crates.

215

C6
HANDLE WITH CARE

HopLow & Family

Designer Quarch Atelier

HopLow is a character in the Disney film *Fantasia*. The underlying idea of the project is "will happiness find us?" Drawing inspiration from work by the artists Peter Fischli and David Weiss, Hoplow & Family is made of borosilicate glass joined together by a simple system that enables interaction with the object. The craftsmanship is highlighted by the blown glass technique, which makes every piece unique.

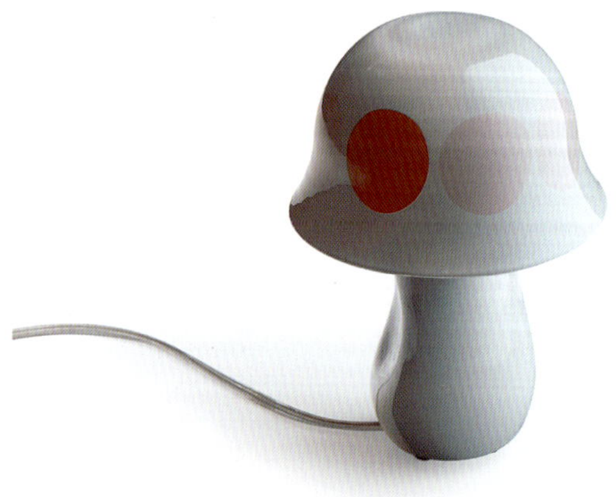

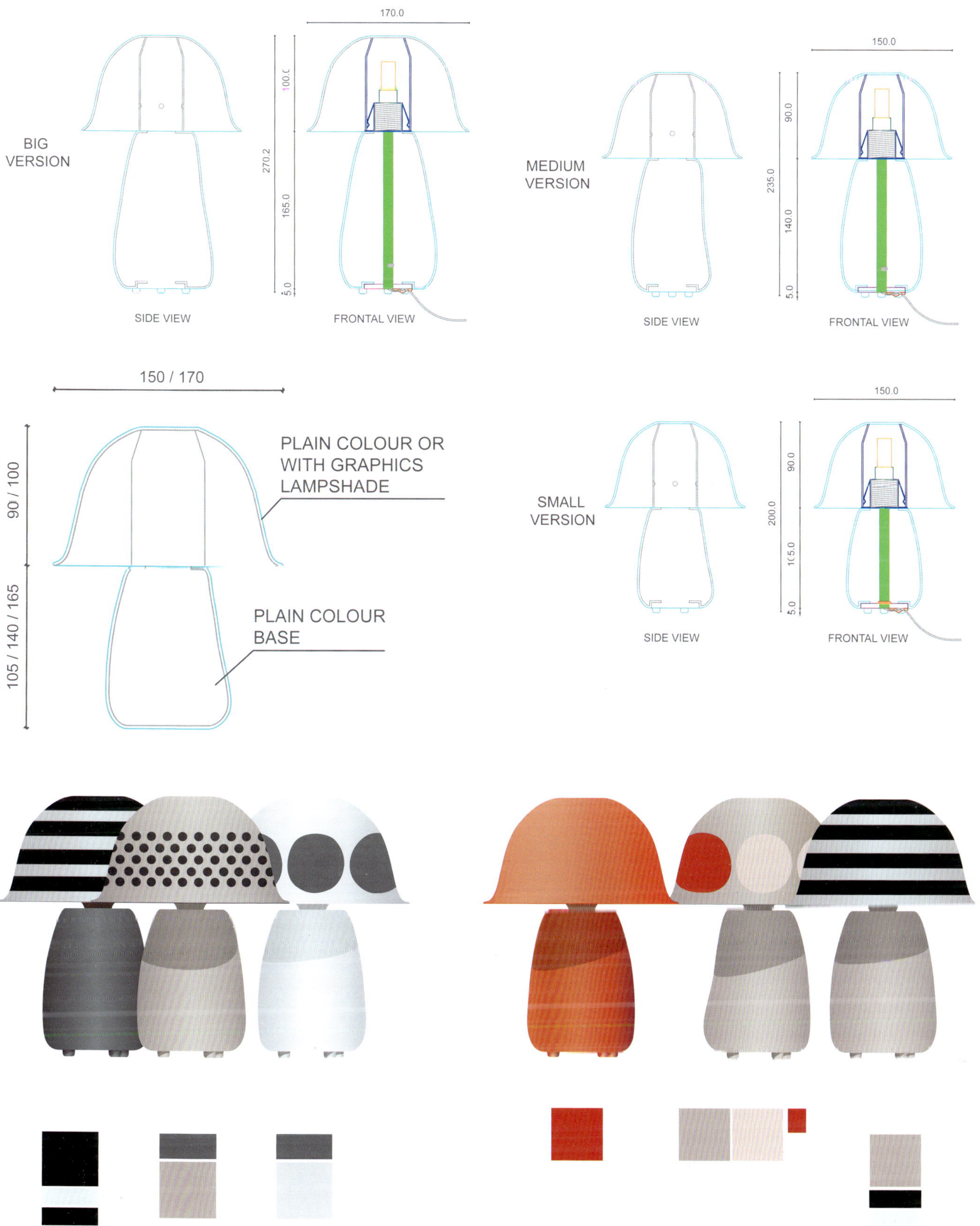
BIG
VERSION
SIDE VIEW
FRONTAL VIEW
170.0
100.0
270.2
165.0
5.0
MEDIUM
VERSION
150.0
90.0
235.0
140.0
5.0
SIDE VIEW
FRONTAL VIEW
150 / 170
90 / 100
105 / 140 / 165
PLAIN COLOUR OR
WITH GRAPHICS
LAMPSHADE
PLAIN COLOUR
BASE
SMALL
VERSION
150.0
90.0
200.0
105.0
5.0
SIDE VIEW
FRONTAL VIEW

Monkey Lamp

Designer Marcantonio Raimondi Malerba

Made of resin and finished by hand, the Monkey Lamp series depicts a monkey in three different positions, exploring the environment with an LED lamp in hand. Like the designer's other work, it is inspired by the relationship between man and nature, and looks for a simple but ironic result.

Hanging Leaves

Studio In Every Tree

Hanging Leaves was inspired by the tree davidia involucrata, commonly known as the handkerchief tree. The designers aimed to bring the beauty of this flowering tree into our homes by hand making a pendant light. Casted in bone china, every detail of the real leaves is precisely captured.

Bike Balls

Designer Scott Bodaly & Heather Lam

Bike Balls are rear bike lights designed to be mounted on the back of the bike seat, and they feature two major innovations that increase cyclists' visibility. An LED was placed inside a silicone shell so that the whole housing glows, which increases the illuminated area from 18 mm^2 to 1872 mm^2. The second innovation is the movement of the light. The design of the housing means that the light bounces around on the back of the seat. This random movement is more noticeable than a static light. The power button was integrated into the silicone, simplifying the assembly.

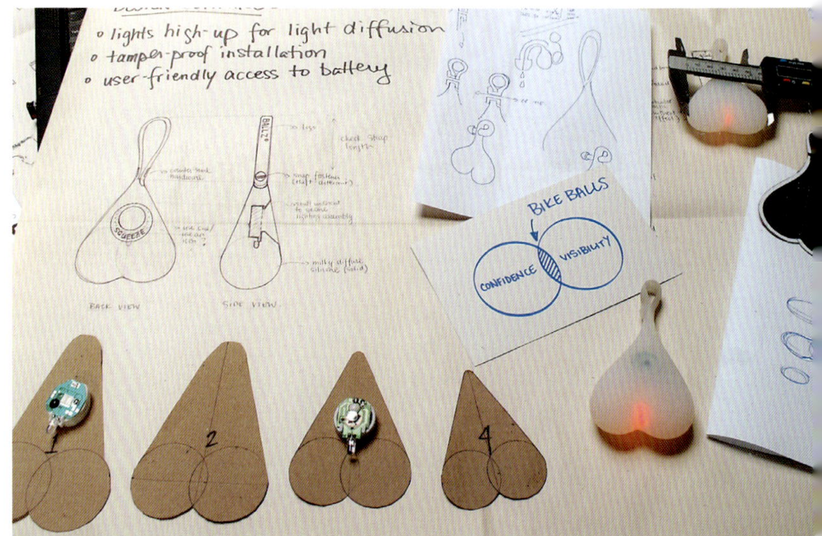

Swarm Lamp

Studio Jangir Madaddi Design Bureau

The genius of the Swarm Lamp lies in its accurate capture of a suspended motion. Specialty Bulbrite light bulbs that reveal the entwined filaments are connected to custom-cut wood that resonates with the Scandinavian design. The angle of each Swarm can be adjusted to a wide range of positions. The Swarm Lamp brings together three simple materials—glass, wood, and metal—as if designed by nature itself.

Onion Vases

Studio AMAI designlab

The Onion Vases were inspired by observations of bulbous plants. The bulb is a symbol of the life of a flower, and the consumer decides what type of flower this "bulb" would become. Like natural flower bulbs, these hand-painted ceramic vases have adopted different shapes and sizes relating to the natural form of the onion, and are even more lively in pairs or clusters.

designlab
ONION VASES

Celestial

Designer Artonomos

Celestial is a series of 3D-printed ceramic lamps. The pattern of holes on each lamp is unique, and bears its own serial number. It comes with a programmed lighting mode, which gently alternately dims and brightens.

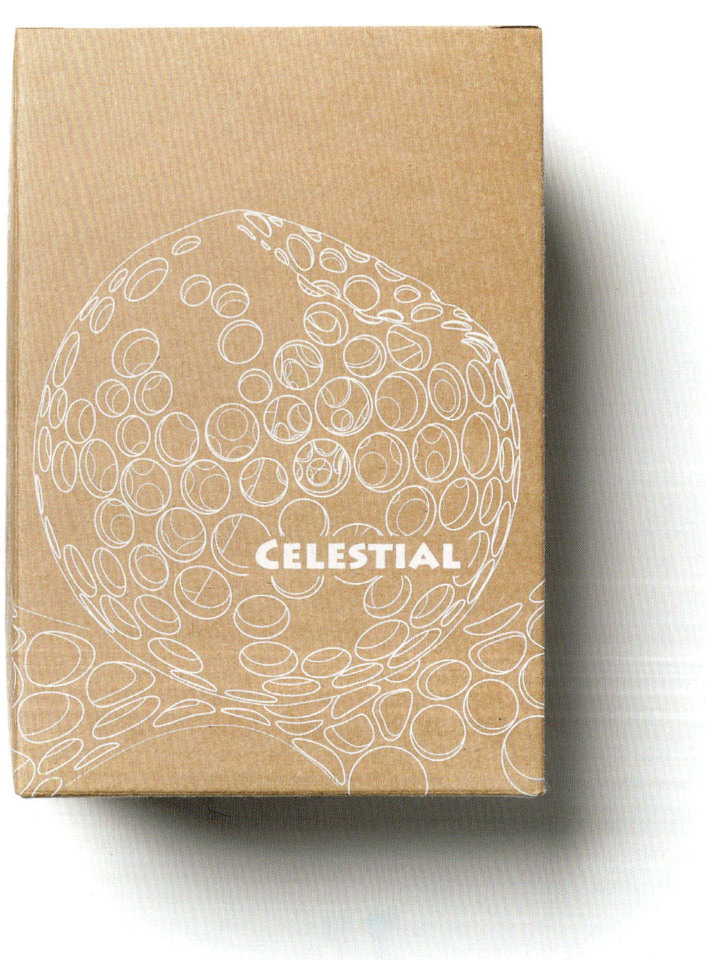

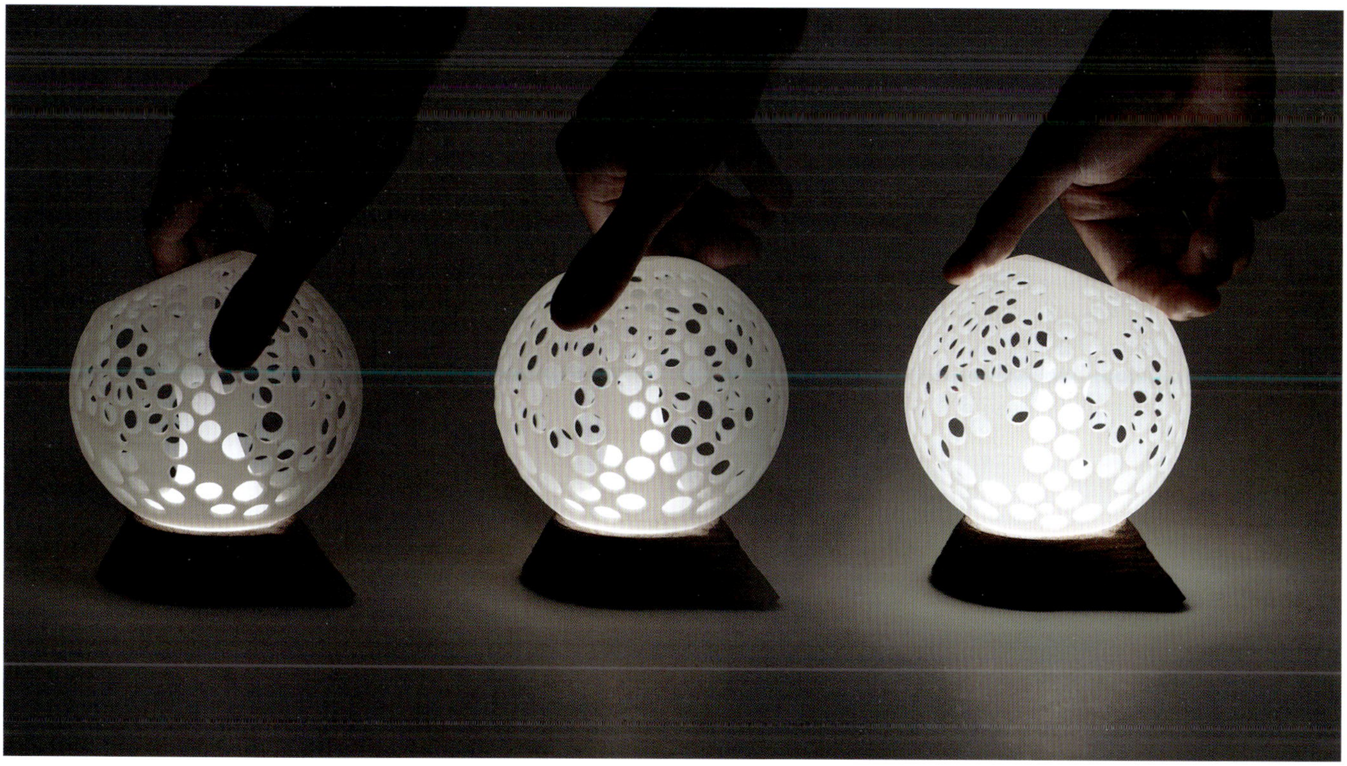

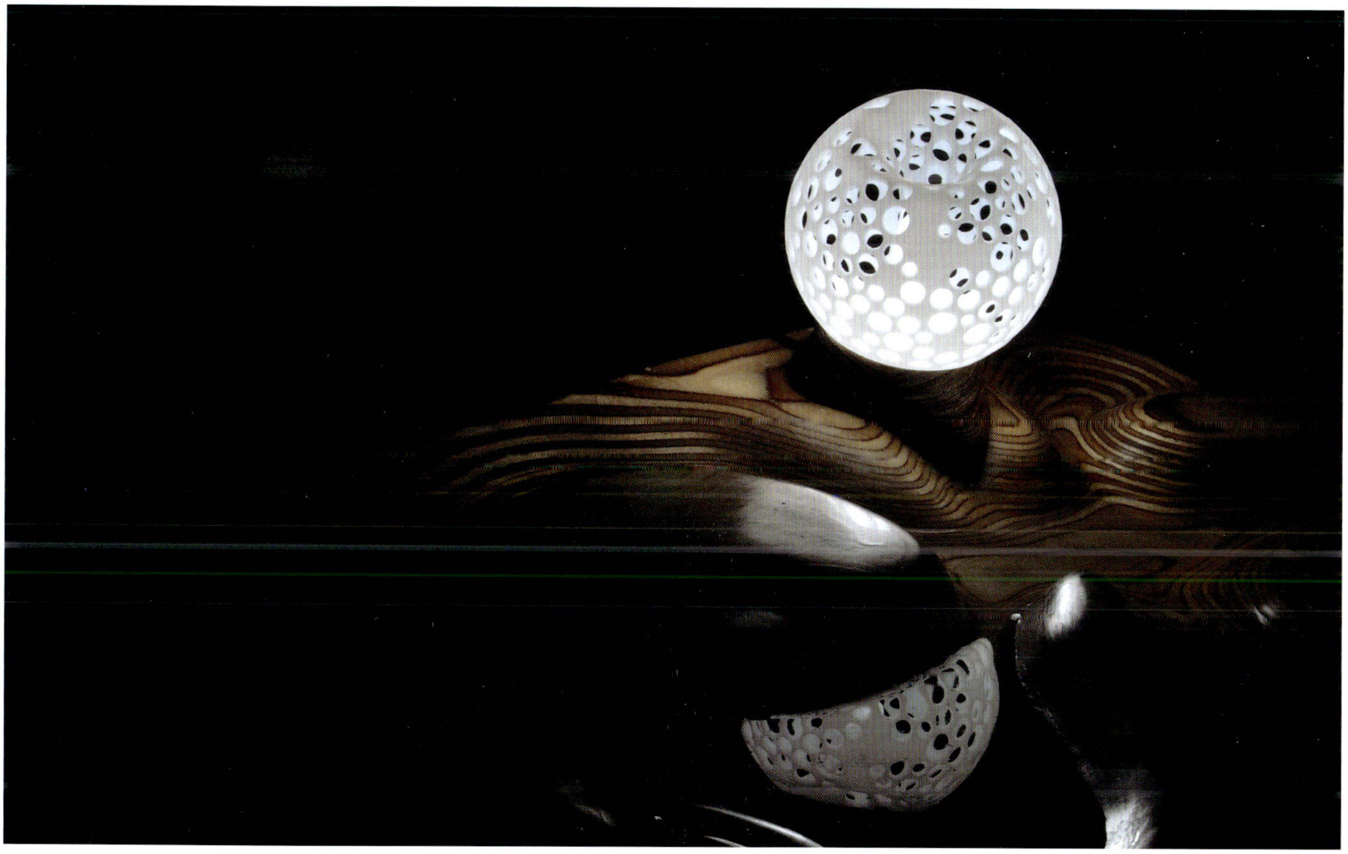

Kuro-Satsuma cs008

Studio nendo

This bowl is characterized by a citrus fruit motif with a transparent glaze finish, incorporating the distinctive black used in Satsuma earthenware, which comes from the iron in the clay and glaze. By applying the glossy glaze just to the inside, it also mimics the refreshing juice of the fruit, while the matted finish outside resembles the peel. Furthermore, the uneven surface of the inside allows the glaze to look different from different perspectives.

○ Form ○

Mt. Mudeung Tea Table & Plate

Studio NOTHING dESIGN GROUP

Designer Koo, Jin-woog

This project is a special souvenir for Mt. Mudeung national park, located in Gwang-ju City, Korea. The transparent acrylic tea table and plate depict an aerial view of Mt. Mudeung through sculpture. The surface is printed with a graphic of Seoseokdae, the columnar jointing of Mt. Mudeung, and a poem about the mountain.

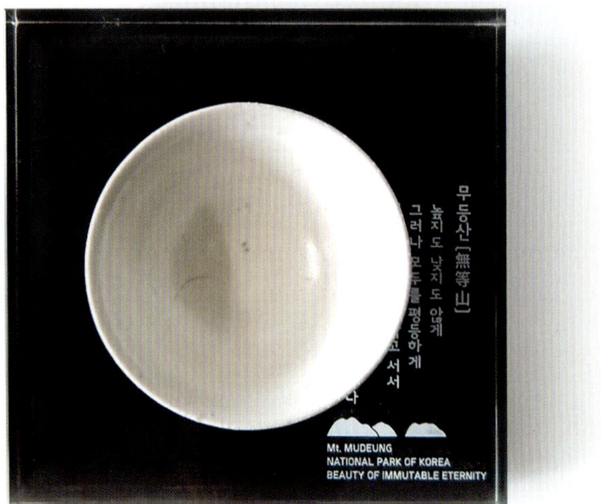
무등산 [無等山]
높지 도 낮지 도 않게
그러나 모두를 평등하게
Mt. MUDEUNG
NATIONAL PARK OF KOREA
BEAUTY OF IMMUTABLE ETERNITY

Seoseokdae Cruet & Vase Set

Studio NOTHING dESIGN GROUP

This design follows the morphology of Seoseokdae, a columnar jointing of Mt. Mudeung in Korea. The cruets and vases are identically shaped but of varied heights so that different combinations can be created to suit personal taste.

Sea of Clouds

Studio NOTHING dESIGN GROUP

This white and black design was inspired by the scenery of Mt. Mudeung in Korea, where the mountain summits seem to be floating in a sea of clouds. Apart from being a decorative ceramic art piece, it can be used as a paperweight in the middle size and as a chopstick rest in the small size.

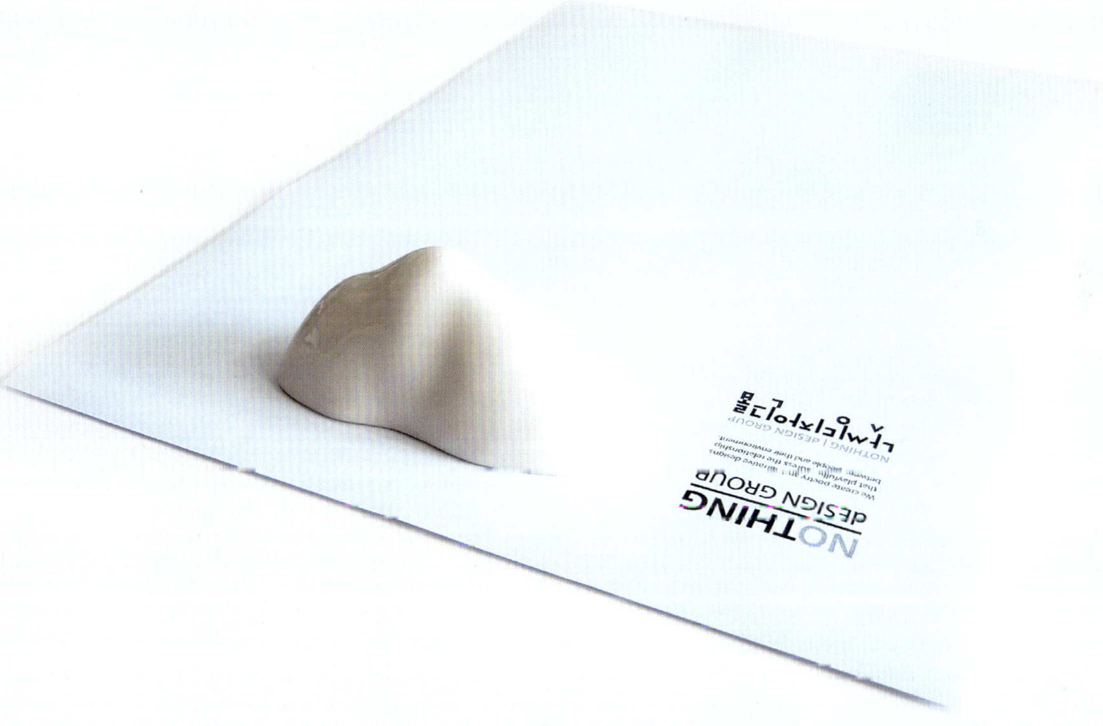

Form

Pirouet

Studio KDID

Designer Malte Koslowski, Georg Dwalischwili

The project was born out of a fascination with lens apertures. After much testing and refinement, a blossom-shape was acquired, adding a natural beauty to the design. The lamp has variable settings, creating a unique choreography of light and shadow.

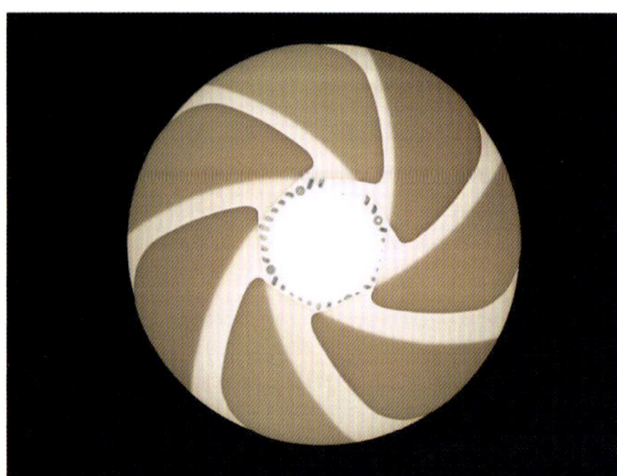

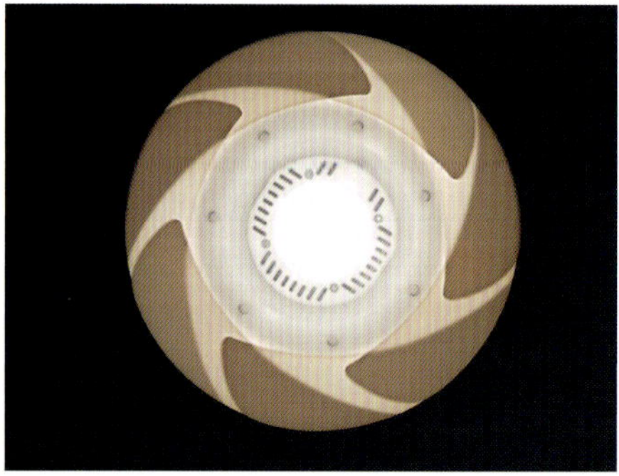

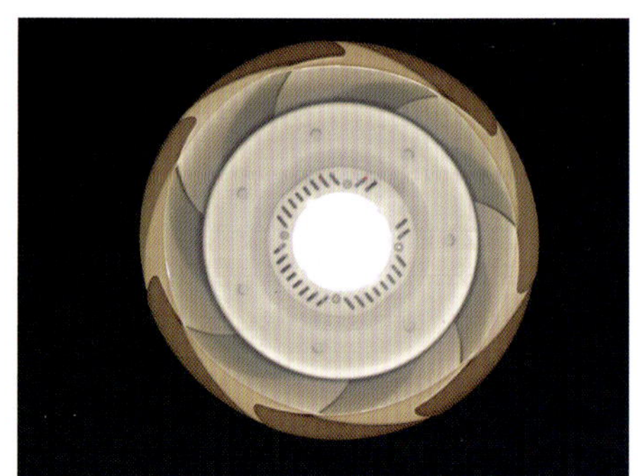

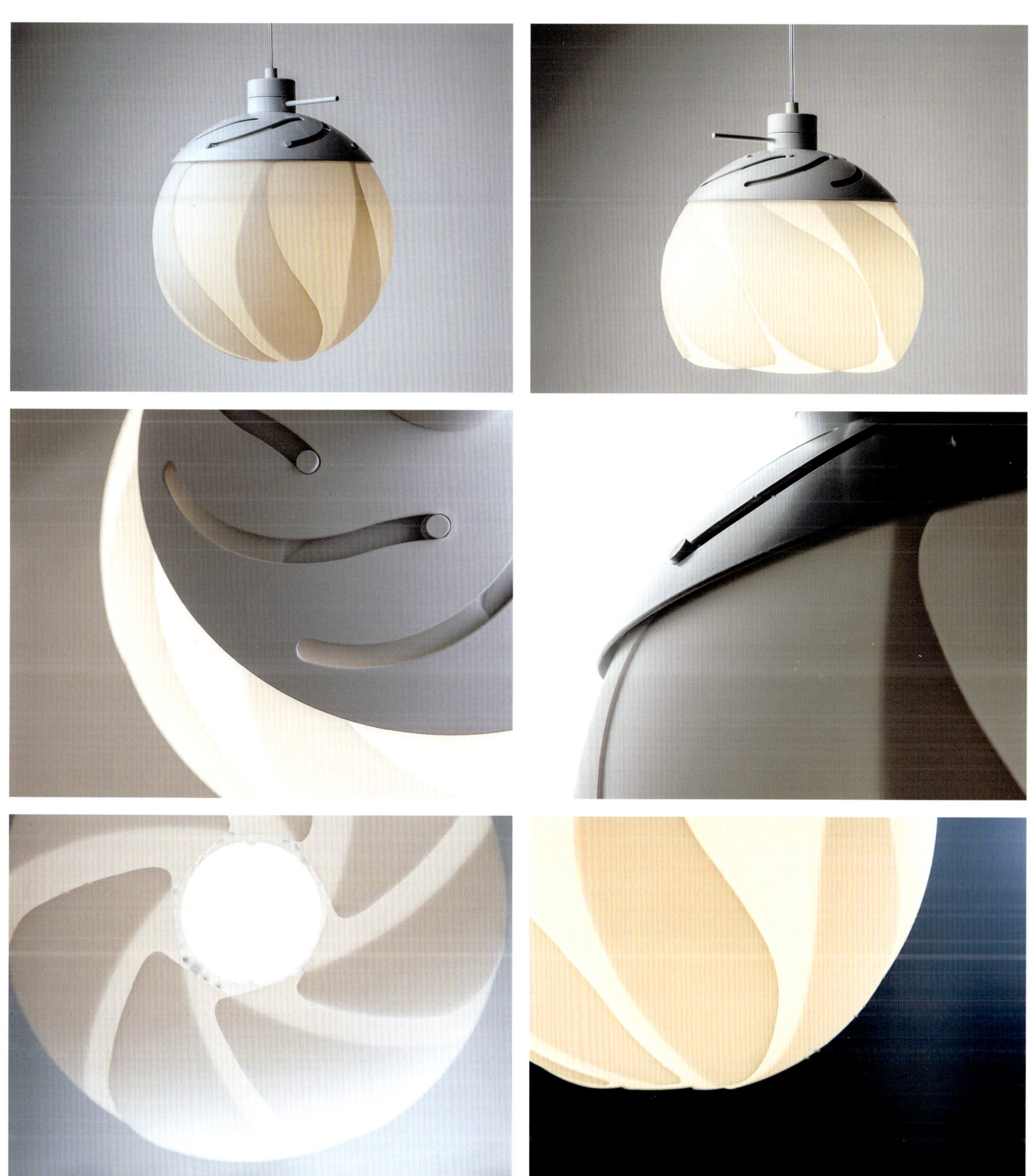

Form

Octopus Chandeliers

Designer Adam Wallacavage

Over a decade ago, Wallacavage first began experimenting with chandeliers for the dining room of his Victorian brownstone that were inspired by the classic novel *Twenty Thousand Leagues under the Sea*. To construct his original octopus chandeliers, he learned the traditional techniques of ornamental plastering, which involves casting and hand-sculpting with epoxy clay and resin. In the years since, he has continued to experiment with form, color and technique, developing his own unique glazes, vibrant hues and finishes.

Coral

Studio David Trubridge Studio

The structure of the pendant light is based on a geometric polyhedron. Its intricate form is made of just a single component repeated sixty times. Originally designed purely as an experiment, it only became a light later when the designer tried to find a use for it by putting a bulb inside. Coral comes in 6 sizes. The plywood finish can be all natural or painted on one side, thus creating a stock selection of 11 options, including black.

Floral

Studio David Trubridge Studio

Also based on a geometric polyhedral form, Floral was designed to be a softer, more decorative offering that complements Coral light. Floral comes in 6 sizes. The plywood finish can be all natural or painted on one side, thus creating a stock selection of 11 options, including black.

Kōura

Studio David Trubridge Studio

Kōura pendant light was inspired by woven baskets and also by the curled form of the New Zealand native fresh water shrimp, kōura, which is its Māori name. Kōura comes in 6 sizes. The plywood finish can be all natural, caramel or painted on one side, thus creating a stock selection of 11 options, including black.

Kina

Studio David Trubridge Studio

Kina pendant light references the inner shell of the local salt water sea-urchin called kina in Maori. Kina comes in 5 sizes. The plywood finish can be all natural or painted on one side, thus creating a stock selection of 11 options, including black.

Flounce

Desinger Artonomos

Flounce is a unique 3D-printed pendant light. The folds on each lamp shade are different. The light can be used as a group or as single piece to create an organic, peaceful atmosphere for your dining area or bedroom. The shade filters the light gently to give a soft illumination.

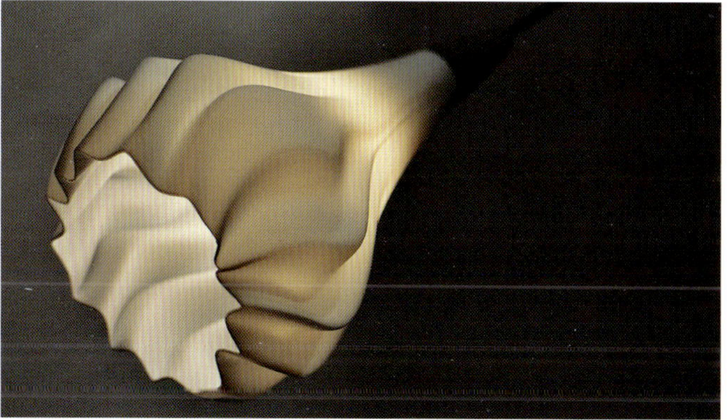

FLOUNCE
Artonomos Ltd
16H, Fu Cheung Centre, Shatin, H.K.
© 2014 Artonomos Ltd.
All Rights reserved.

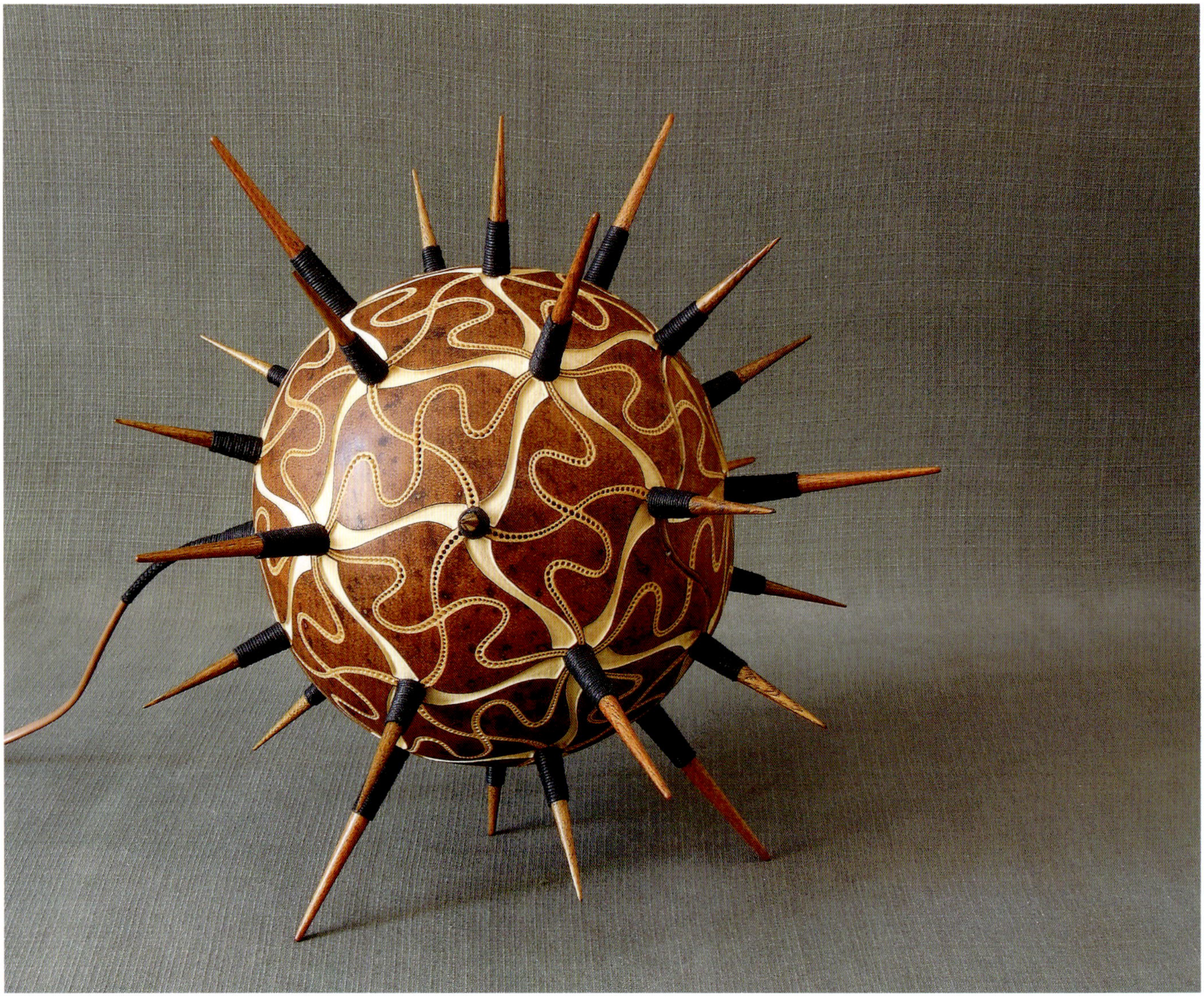

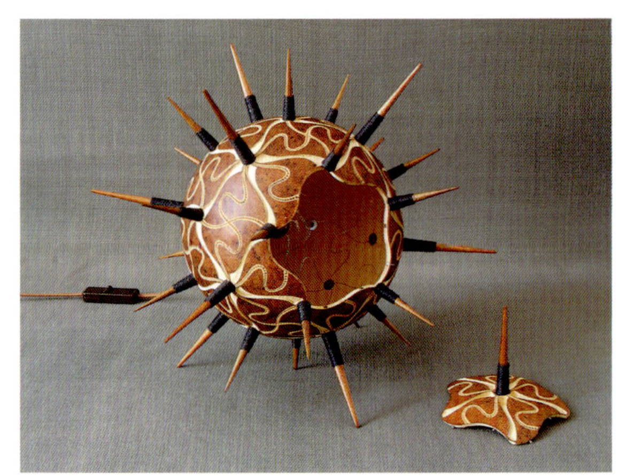

Table Lamp XIII—Thorn Sphere

Designer Przemek Krawczyński

Made of Senegalese gourd, this fully handcrafted lamp was inspired by some of the spherical, spiked forms found in nature. The pattern on the sphere is made of the base of a dodecahedron. The thorns are carved from oak wood, painted with natural oil and finished with black waxed cord. The white carvings, which reveal a deeper layer of white wood, allow some light to pass through. The lamp's opening is fastened with small magnets.

At Your Command

Designer Daniel Loves Objects

At Your Command is a movable mannequin lamp that allows your imagination to run wild by challenging the conventions of a classical lamp. The mannequin's joints can be moved into different postures. Finished in gold plating to give a touch of exquisiteness, the product has two different sizes: 1.7 m and 0.8 m when fully standing.

○ Form ○

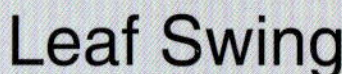

Leaf Swing

Studio MUT Design

Inspired by fallen leaves and made of laminated material, Leaf Swing is a suspended swing seat for adults.
It can be used outdoors or indoors and features an interesting leaf shadow created by the sunlight.

Fly Push Pin

Studio Suck UK

Designer Funtastic Plastic

Fly push-pins are a practical joke and a practical holder of photos and ticket stubs around the house. They are a great gift for any pteronarcophobic.

suckUK
push
pins
24 push pins
punaises

Leaf Hooks

Studio Suck UK

Designer Hwa Jin, Jung

The Leaf Hooks were designed to add some functional greenery to dull empty walls. They can be used to hang small household items such as keys, tea-towels and pictures.

Leaf Hooks
X6
NAIL COVERS
suckUK

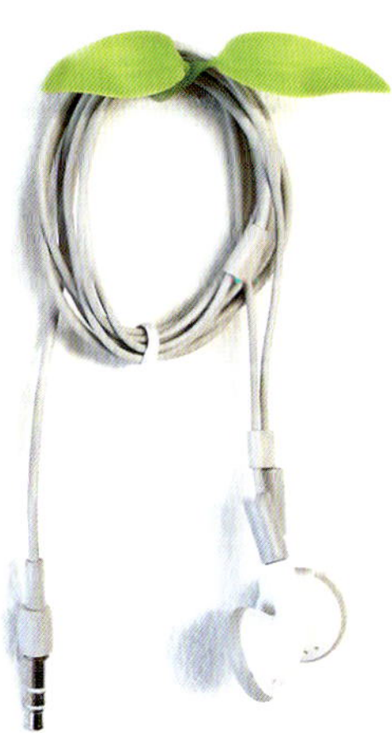

Thumb Drives

Designer Justin Poulsen

Specialized in building physical props, the designer created "thumb" drives loaded with his portfolio, allowing potential clients to experience both the tactile and visual qualities of his craft.

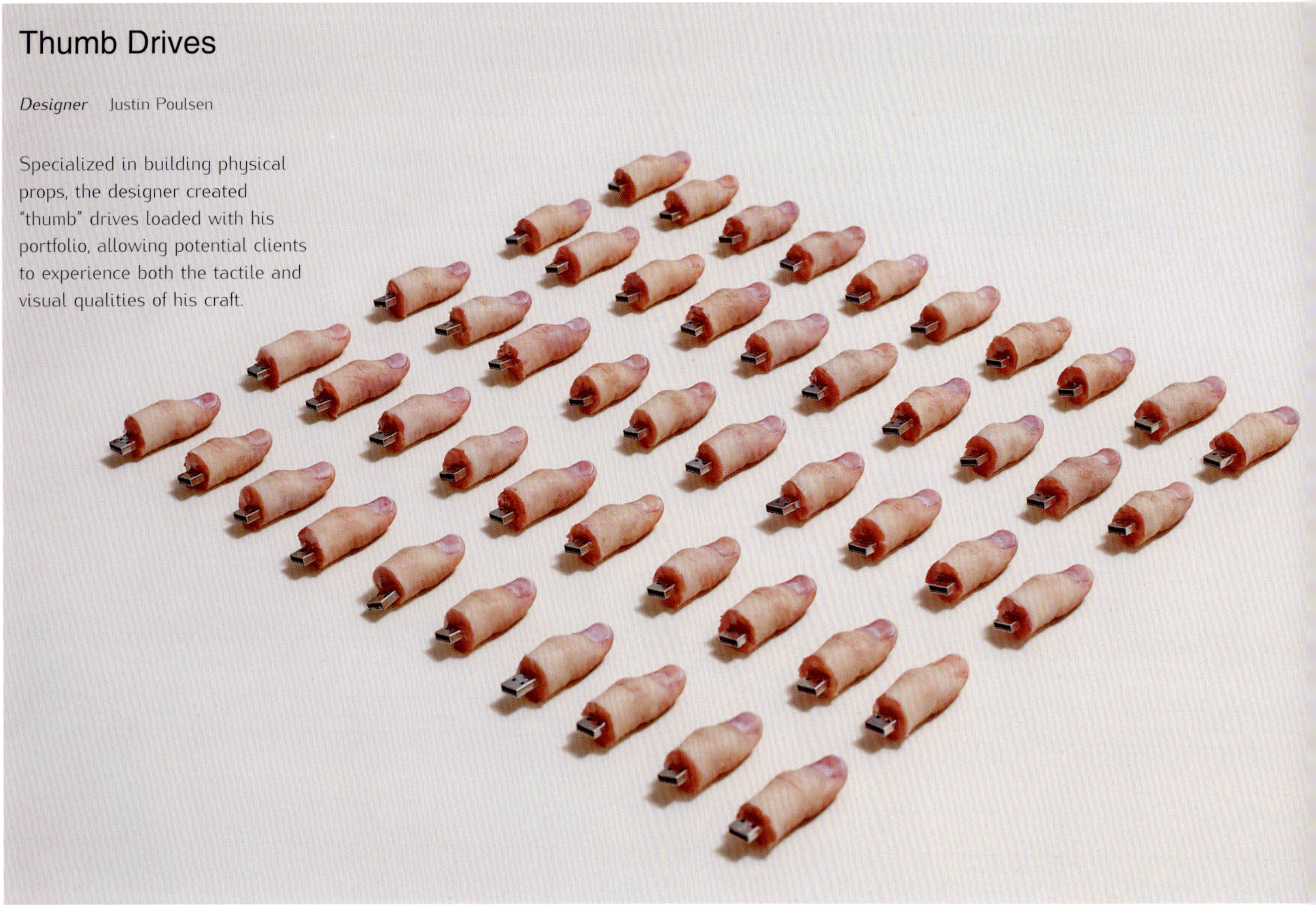

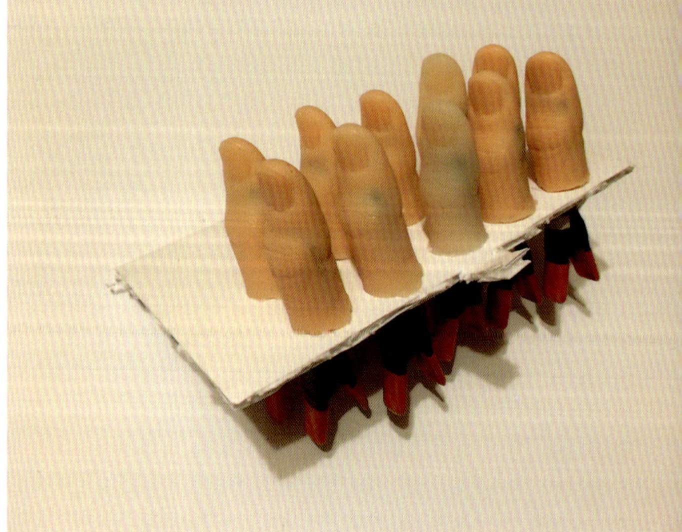

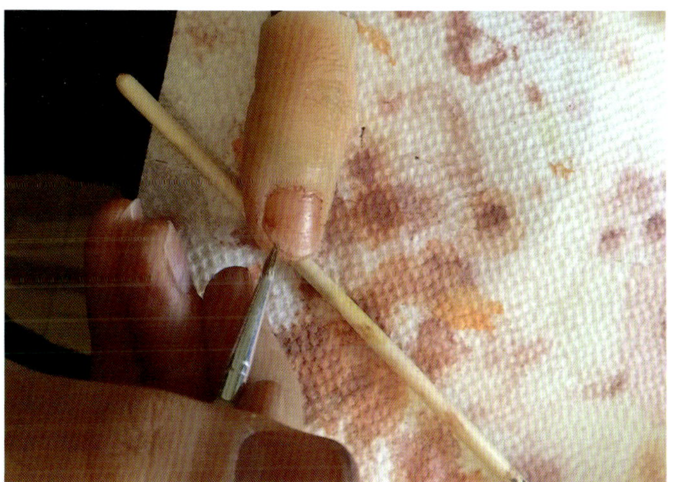

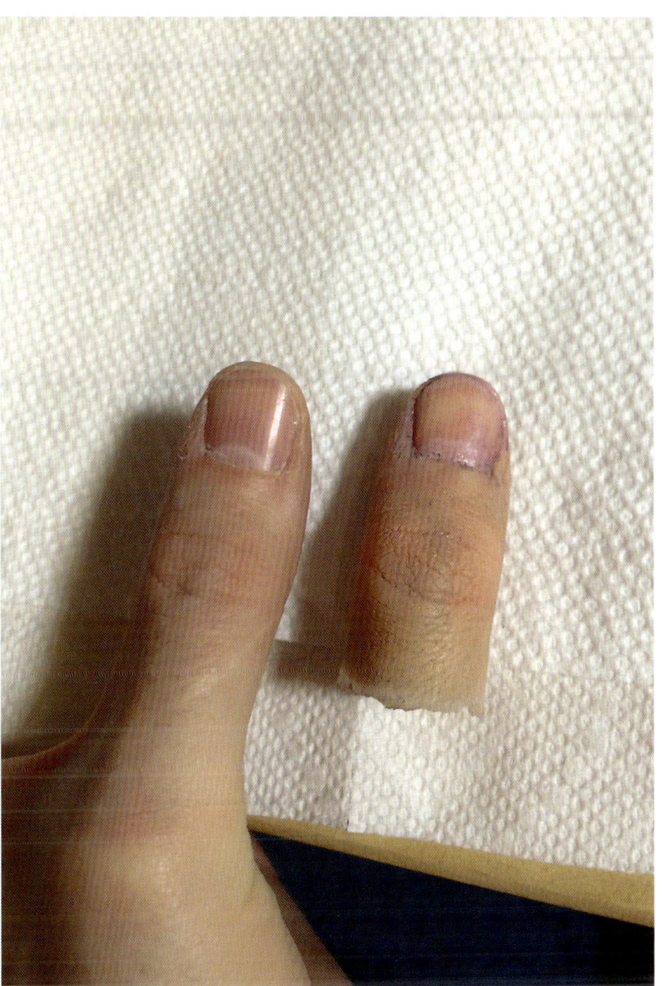

Stick out like a sore thumb.
JUSTIN POULSEN PHOTOGRAPHY
647.966.6347 / J@JUSTINPOULSEN.COM / JUSTINPOULSEN.COM

Black Swan

Designer Nir Meiri

Inspired by the elegant posture of a black swan, this lamp imitates its head-tilting movement with its rotating parts. At the same time, the outline of the movement is cast in the light, like a reflection on the surface of water.

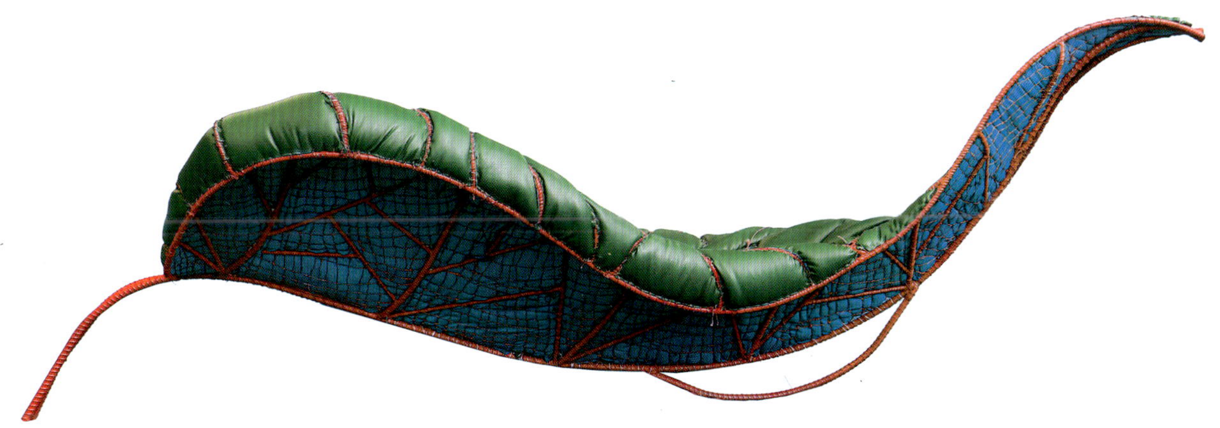

Bomers' nr. 2

Designer Jeroen Bomers

The Bomers' nr. 2 is a sofa that simulates a fallen leaf settled gracefully on the earth. The hand-curved steel frame of the structure follows the same pattern as the veins of the greenery, adopting its natural structure and strength. The skeleton is surrounded by specially crafted leather-clad cushioning, while the "veins" of the seat are left exposed for a pronounced aesthetic of contrasting colors.

Rain Lamp

Studio Richard Clarkson Studio

This design consists of a large clear globe at the top of which is an encased micro-peristaltic pump and LED light bulb and at the bottom of which lies a pool of lightly chlorinated water. The hidden pump circulates water from the pool and releases droplets that fall around the bulb. As the droplets fall on the pool, the light refracts on the surface of the water, disturbed by the ripples. The inherent shape of the globe acts as a magnifying lens that projects the effect on the surface below and creates a very subtle rainbow effect surrounding the projection.

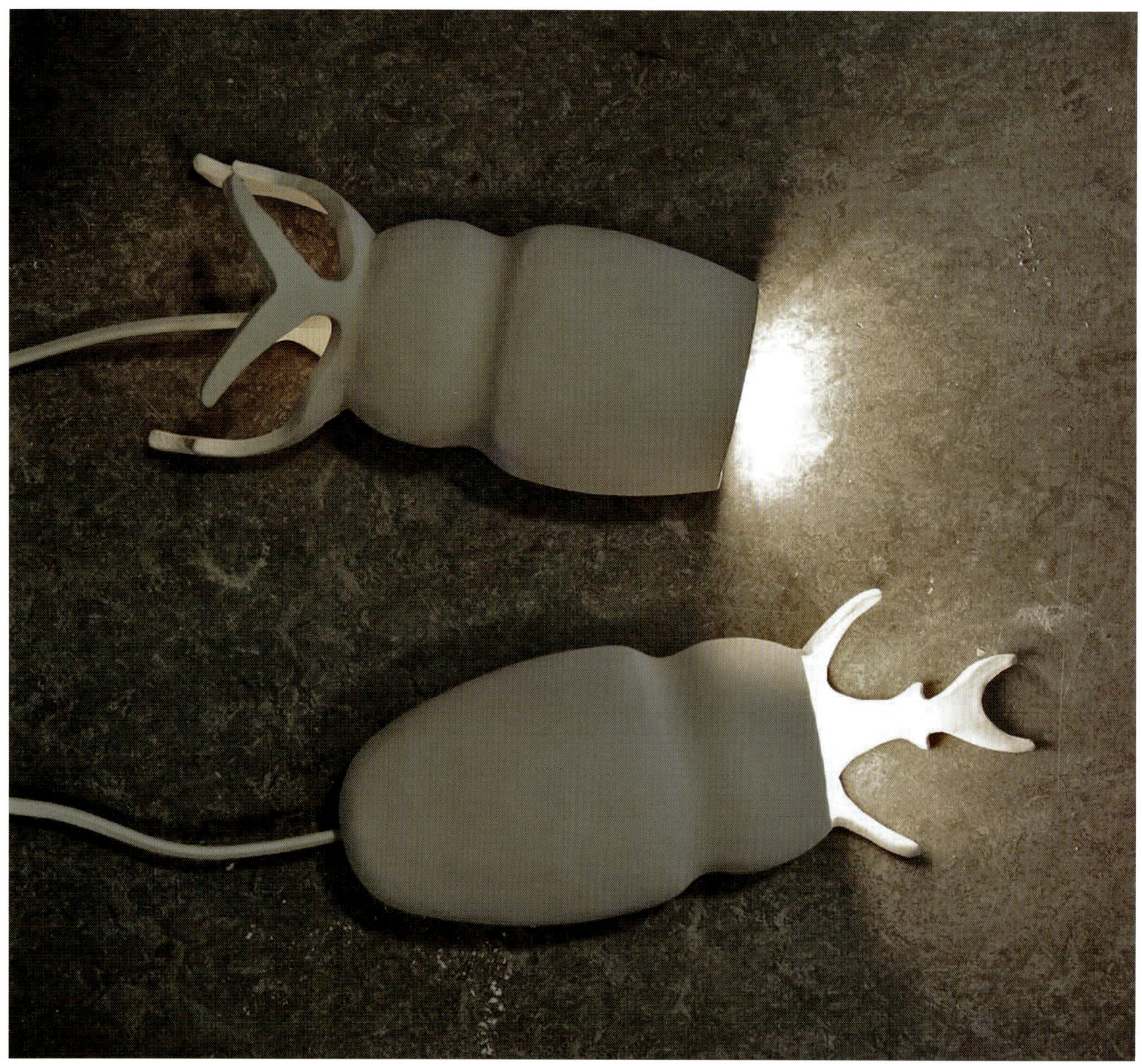

Scarabeo

Designer Francesca Barchiesi

Scarabeo is the Italian word for beetle, referring especially to shiny insects like the Japanese beetle or the gold beetle. The Scarabeo is a porcelain lamp that combines serial production methods with handcrafting interventions that make every piece unique. Once the piece comes out of the mold, the guidelines are imprinted on the soft clay. The final process is to cut out the desired shapes, creating a different type of bug every time. The bottom part can be cut out to create a second opening for the light.

Tiny Cloud

Studio Richard Clarkson Studio

Tiny Cloud was specifically designed to be the "little brother" of the Smart Cloud. It can either be used in tandem or as a stand-alone piece. Staying true to the original Smart Cloud, the Tiny Cloud features an LED reactive Bluetooth speaker, an ambient light mode and a new "demo mode" which allows the user to experience all the features simultaneously.

Form

Hidden Animals Mug Collection

Studio imm Living

Designer Ange-line Tetrault

This series of porcelain mugs adds a surprise to a tea party. The animals are initially hidden under the tea and are revealed as the cup is drained. Perfect for hot or cold beverages, the hidden animals include a fox, an owl and a bear.

○ Form ○

Animal-Inspired

Studio kamina&C

Designer Takeshi Sawada

Chairs can be more than just a piece of furniture and perceived as more than just a means of alleviating physical weariness. Through the utilization of animal motifs and their calming effects, these chairs can elevate one's sense of well-being, providing the users with a relief physically and mentally.

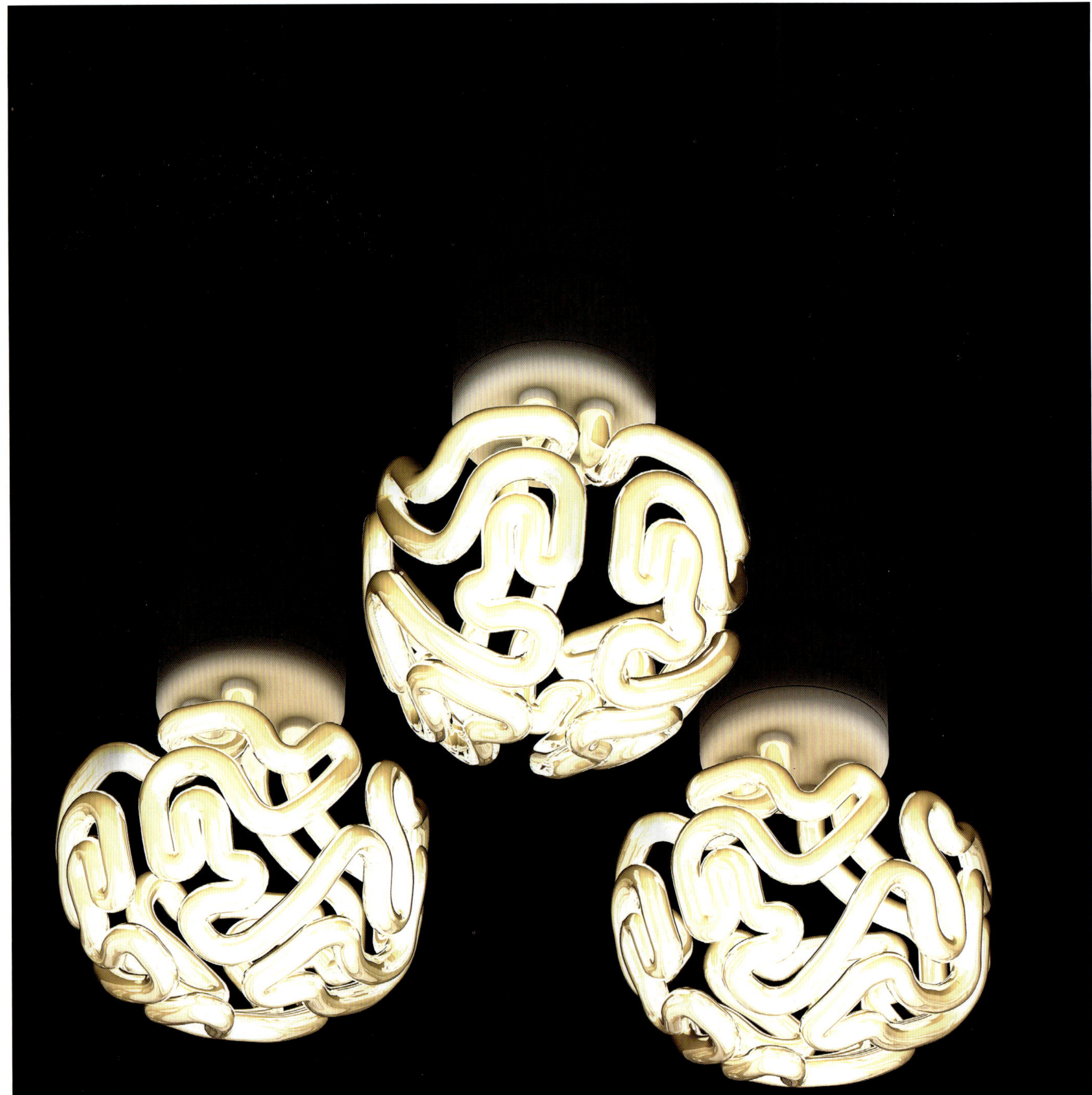

Insight Lamp

Studio Solovyovdesign

Designer Maria and Igor Solovyov

The project plays on the product's classic image as a symbol of a good idea. It is a symbiosis of perfect craft and LED technology.

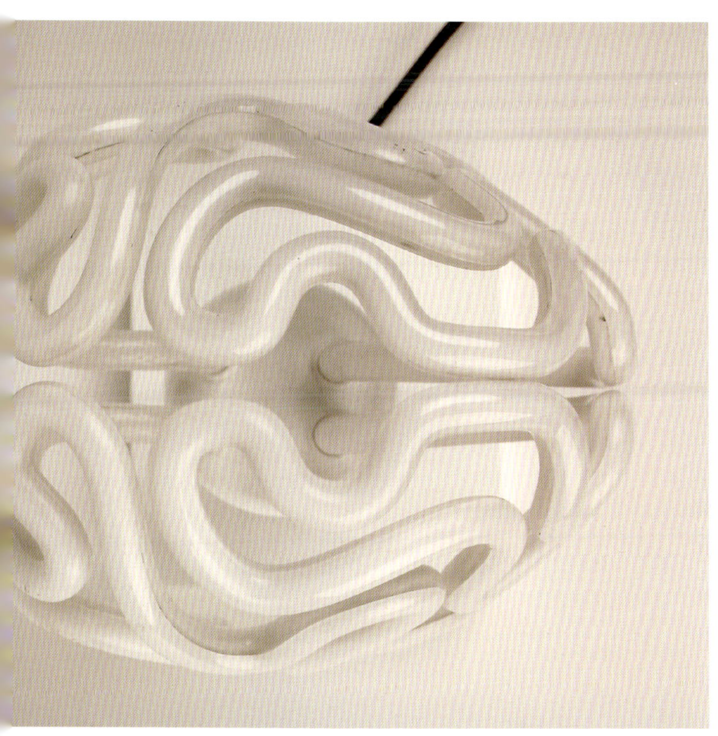
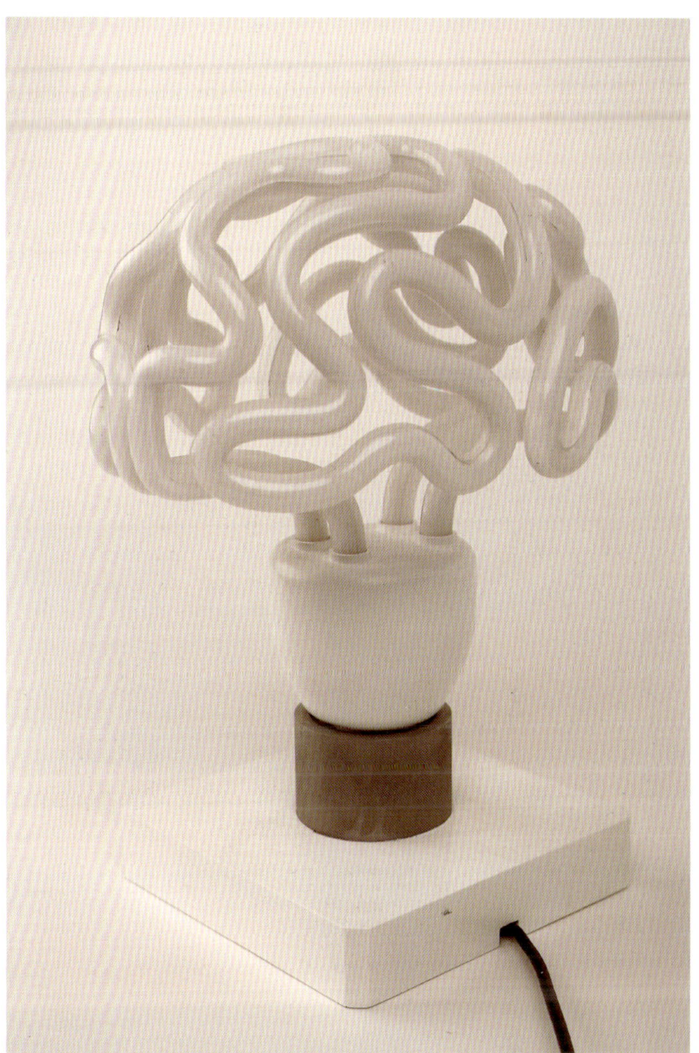
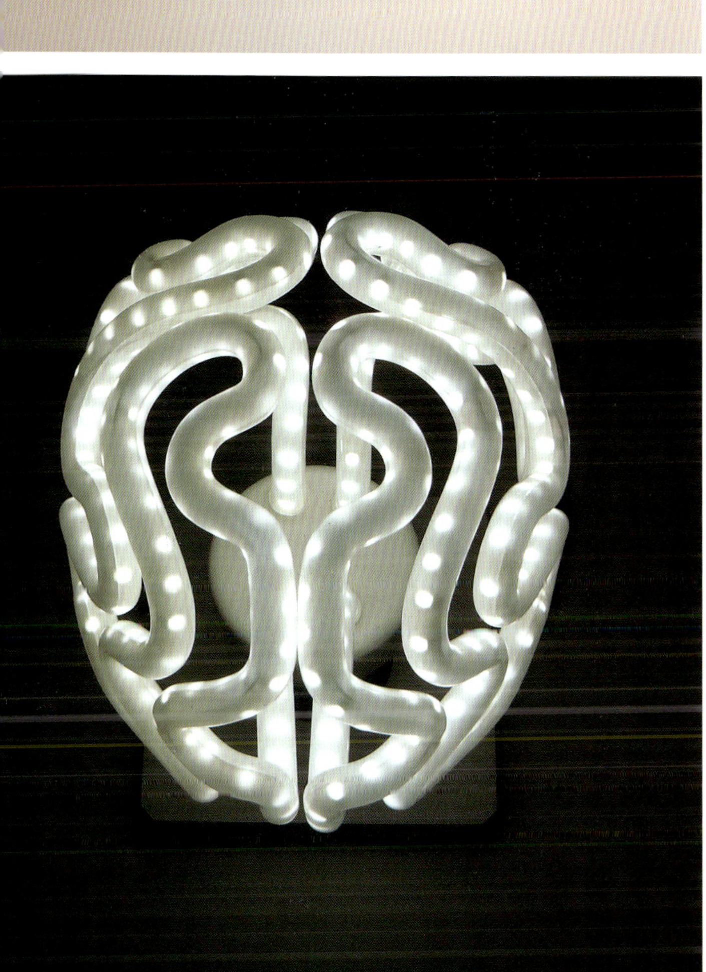

Form

Animal Chairs

Designer Maximo Riera

This collection is a homage to these animals and the whole animal kingdom and an attempt to reflect and capture the beauty of nature that is in each living thing. The Octopus Chair is the first piece of the Animal Chair Collection, and it establishes a base and point of departure for the pieces that follow. The chair contains an internal steel frame to support weight and reinforce the balance.

Cellular Table

Designer Onur Ozkaya

Cellular Table was developed using three different layers of cellular structure to provide lightweight performance. The layers are made of 3D-printed nylon and are hand-finished. Several CAD models have been refined to evaluate certain structural conditions, during which both material thickness and pattern algorithm were adjusted in order to acquire the most structural stability with the least material.

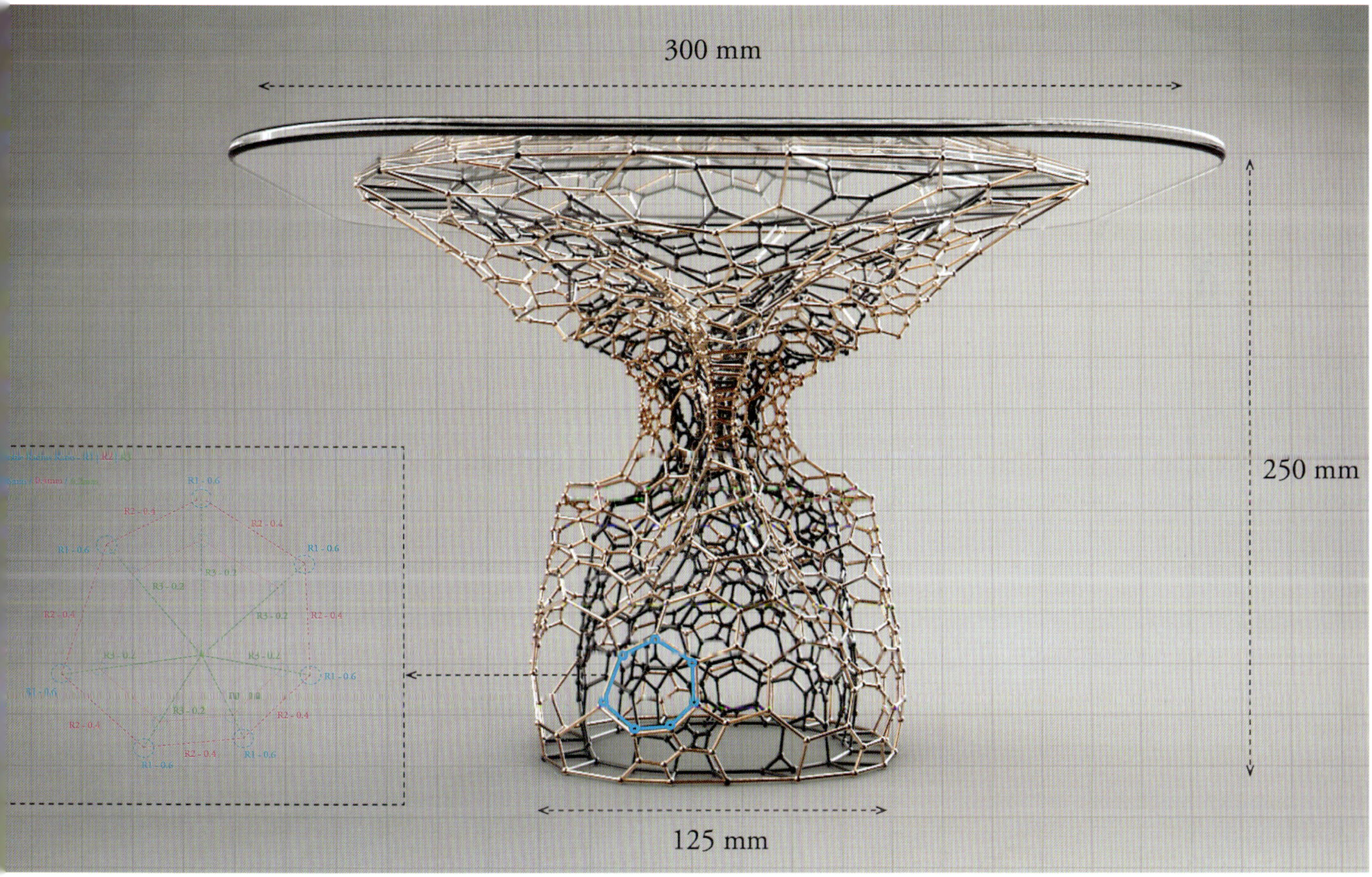

300 mm

250 mm

125 mm

Chip

Designer Rodrigo Torres

Chip is a chrome-plated zamak clip holder. An internal magnet grasps the clips, giving the bird-shaped holder a plumed look. It is exceptionally solid and can also be used as a desktop paperweight.

Kastor

Designer Rodrigo Torres

Studies of the animal's features helped to define accurately the form of the sharpener—a beaver poised to gnaw on the tip of the pencil. Thanks to the solid construction, it also makes an ideal paperweight.

Domestic Animals

Studio Studio DaG

Designer Guus van Leeuwen

Domestic Animals is a series of animal-shaped radiators that refer to a time when people lived with their livestock and used animal furs for warmth. More than just a radiator, it is intended to draw people together like a fireplace in home. The removable furs on the heating are filled with wheat kernels which retain warmth.

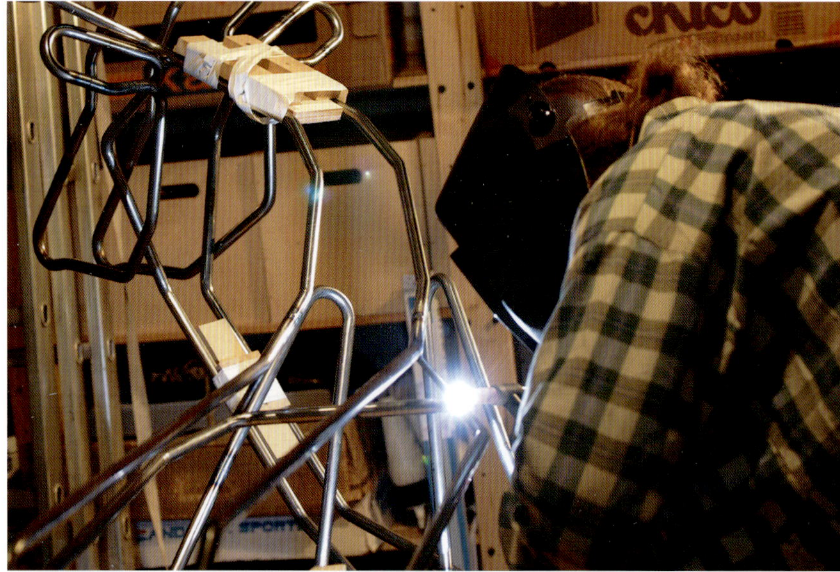

○ Form ○

Flower Lamps

Designer Laszlo Tompa

These cherry wood pendant lamps are the result of the designer's many years of geometric experiments. The basic lamp is a hexagonal and pentagonal pyramid which is covered with different matching geometric ornaments. Due to the special constructions, several unique flower shapes were formed.

I Got Brain—Candle Holder

Studio Brainfart55

Designer Bao

This playful candle holder holds small candles and incense cones with a diameter of up to 4 cm. The upper and lower parts of the holder and the custom-made brain candles can be freely combined based on personal preference. Replacing the lid to extinguish the candle causes the smoke to come out of the eyes of the holder.

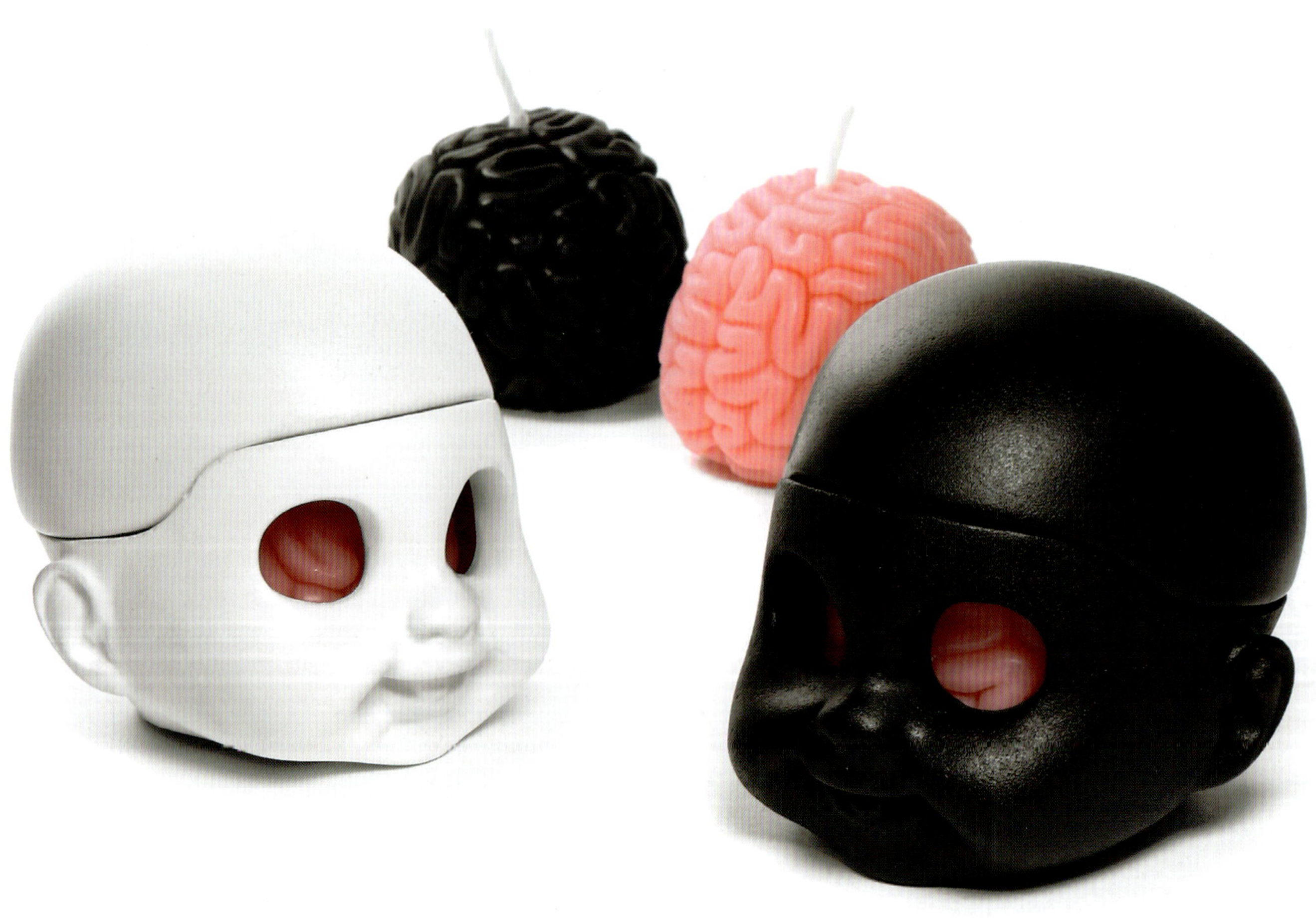

Form

Imatlapalsi

Designer Lisa Dudley

The Imatlapalsi is a sculptural fruit bowl inspired by the lush vegetation found in the mountainous region of Malinalco, Mexico. The name comes from the Nahuatl word for the leaf that inspired the bowl's organic form. The local craftsmen often draw inspiration from the natural shape and grain of the wood, and modify their designs based on what the wood is revealing to them as they work. This is the reason why the designer allowed the bowl to evolve based on the natural form of the wood, leaving some of the texture from the carving process.

Kala Carpet

Designer Maija Puoskari

Kala is a carpet inspired by animal hide rugs, and is intended as a humorous comment by the designer. The carpet is made of ecological felt and can be hung on the wall with a hook. It is suitable for both home and public spaces.

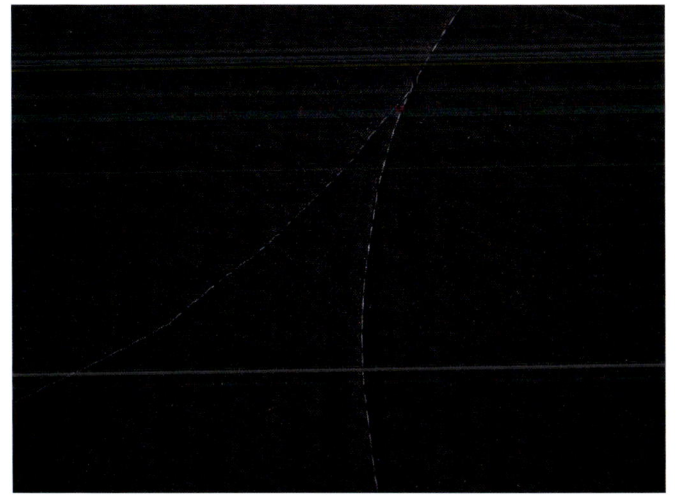

Pyggy Bank

Studio Bureau

Designer Kai Yeo, Yasser Suratman, Edmund Seet

People in the Middle Ages stored their money in jars made from an orange clay called "pygg", which led to the name Pyggy Bank. The project has adopted the form of a life-sized pork leg as an exceptionally fun way of breaking the money box.

Five-Finger Fillet

Designer Raffaele Iannello

The five-finger fillet, also known as the knife game, inspired this collection of stainless steel knives and pens, which are characterized by the presence of a chrome hand resting on a plastic stump. The series includes a set of five kitchen knives, a set of six steak knives and a set of five pens. The pen was intentionally designed to resemble a knife handle.

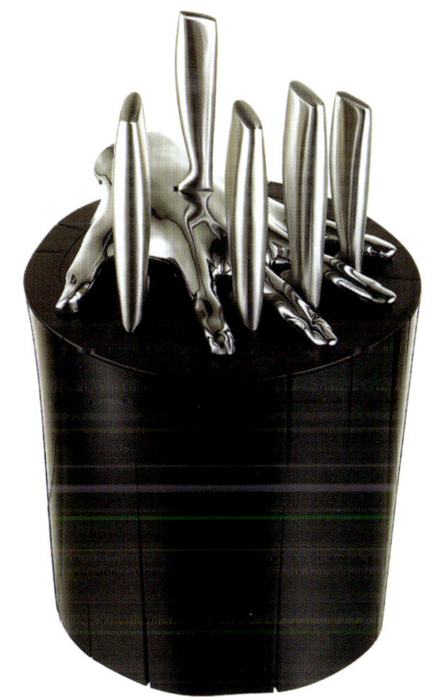

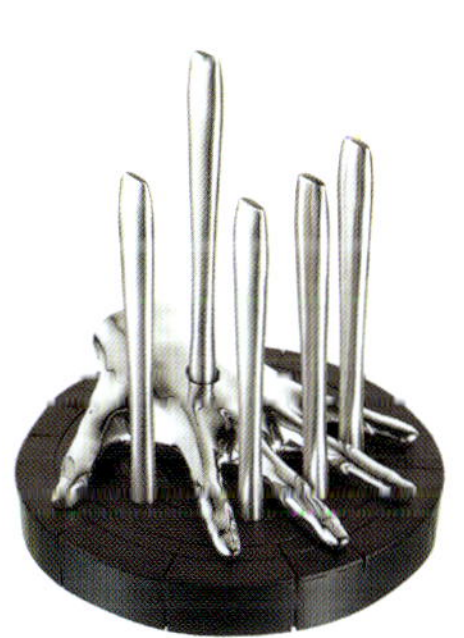

Frozen Peas

Studio Suck UK

Designer Alessandro Martorelli

This giant pea-pod produces ice spheres which melt 80% slower than cube-shaped ice. The ice tray was designed to stay upright to prevent water spilling when it is filled. Once frozen, the ice can be easily squeezed out of the mold.

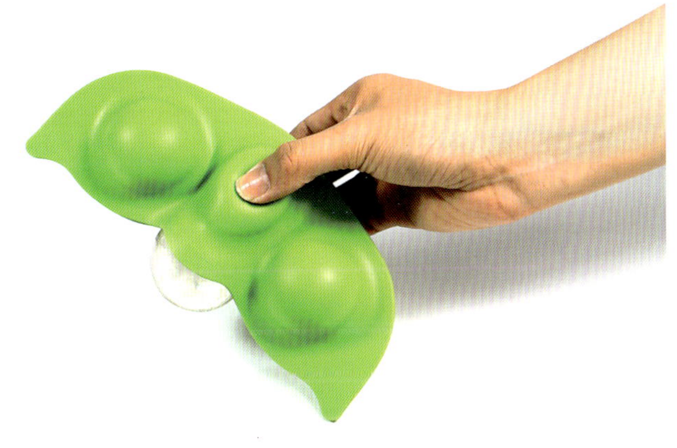

ICE MOULD
FROZENPEAS
ICE CUBE MOULD MAKES ICE BALLS

FROZENPEAS

FROZEN PEAS
ICE MOULD
FROZENPEAS
MOULD MAKES ICE BALLS
FROZENPEAS
MAKES 3 GIANT ICE BALLS
KEEP DRINKS COLDER FOR LONGER

FROZEN PEAS
ICE MOULD
FROZENPEAS
FROZENPEAS
MAKES 3 GIANT ICE BALLS
KEEP DRINKS COLDER FOR LONGER
FROZENPEAS

Shark Lamp

Studio Mukomelov Studio

Designer Aleksandr Mukomelov, Elena Mukomelova

Sharks scare away all creatures around them, but the Shark Lamp only scares away darkness. It is an expressive decorative indoor and outdoor fixture that effectively illuminates the surrounding area.

Veiled Lady

Designer Damien Gernay

This family of table lights, floor lights and chandeliers was inspired by the veiled lady fungus. The production takes advantage of the lost wax casting technique: each piece is sculpted by hand in a wax grid, molded in a ceramic shell and cast in bronze. This allows changing forms to be influenced just by gestural variance.

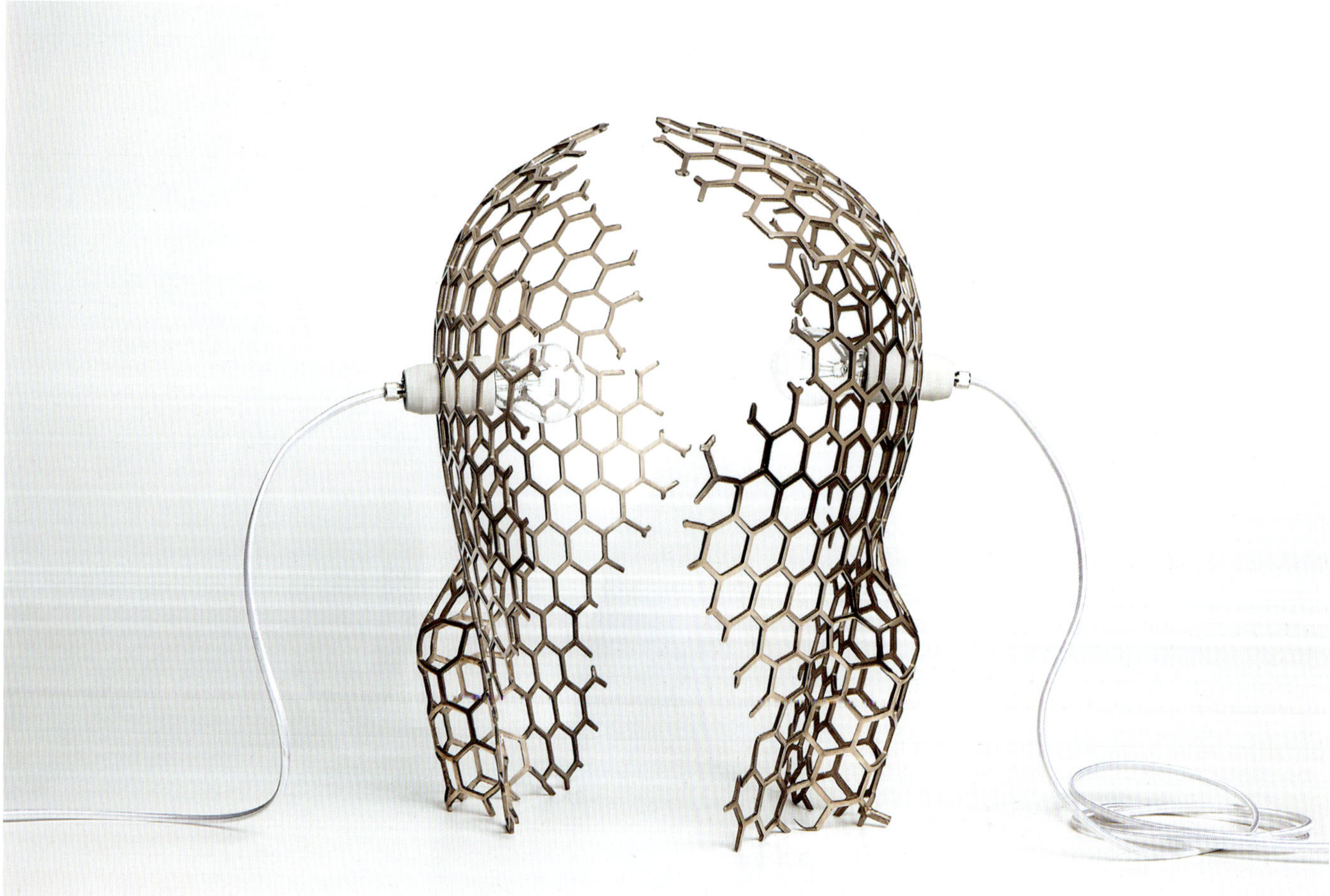

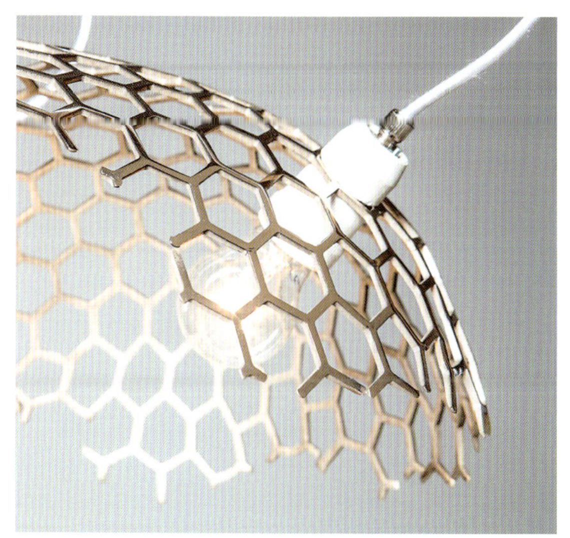

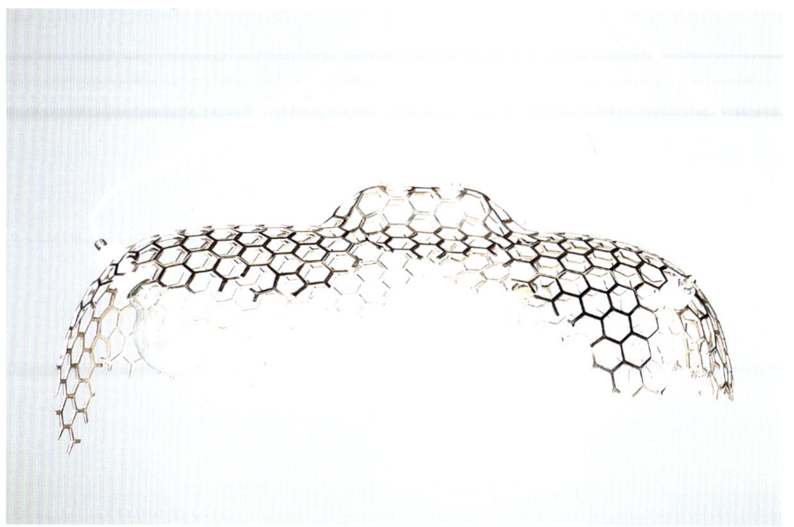

SOULeaf

Studio ilsangisang

Designer Jong su Kim

This collection of leaf lights pays tribute to trees, which purify the environment and infuse our lives with energy. The unique textures of leaves are elaborately silk-screen-printed on environmentally friendly paper. When the lights are turned on in the dark, the animals' silhouettes appear and the leaf-vein patterns become luminous.

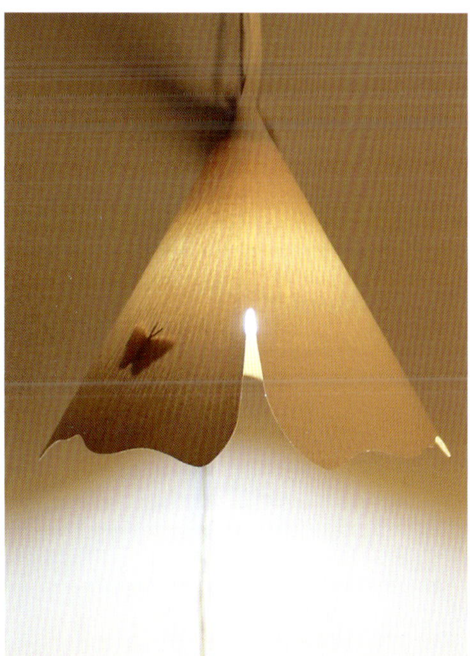

ON LAMP_On Polar Series

Studio ilsangisang

Designer Jong su Kim

This series aims to raise the awareness of environmental protection and of endangered species in the Antarctic and Arctic regions.

Apple Branch

Studio Ayaskan

Following a commission from a dentist's office, the design team took inspiration from the saying "An apple a day keeps the doctor away" to create lighting that is full of life and blends in with the garden outside. The light features 55 glass apples and dangling steel leaves, and its figure is outlined by the LED.

Abyss Table

Studio Duffy London

Designer Christopher Duffy

Like the sea when it deepens, glass darkens when it is layered. The designer wanted to use this effect to replicate a piece of the earth's seabed and experimented with sculpted glass, Perspex and wood. Arranged like a 3D representation of a geological map, the table becomes a geological cross-section of the ocean made out of layers of wood and glass, showing various depths.

ON LAMP_On 4 Seasons

Studio ilsangisang

Designer Jong su Kim

This series of lights is a new concept for the standing lamp, with interchangeable lampshades attached to an LED base using magnets. Made of environmentally friendly paper, the lights bring the four seasons into interior space when they are turned on.

Bionic

Studio Solovyovdesign

Designer Maria and Igor Solovyov

Bionic is a challenging experiment that attempts to turn a biomorphic concept into a reality, taking advantage of both natural structural forms and fluid organic shapes.

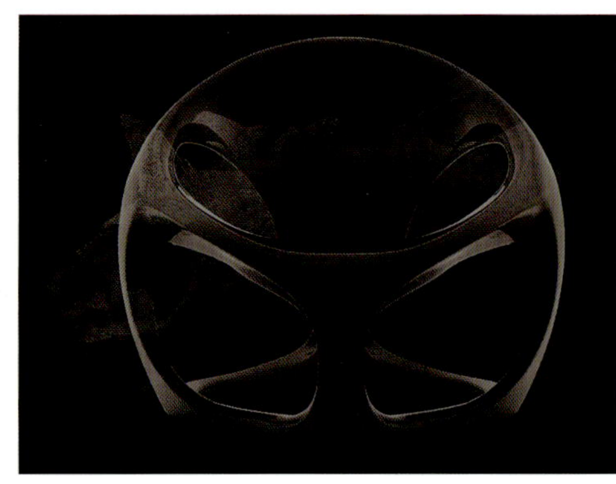

Terho

Studio Mater Design

This series of ceiling lamps was inspired by the natural and likeable shape of the acorn, and are available in three different sizes. The materials include opal white mouth-blown glass and Finnish alder wood.

Selfie Arm

Designer Justin Crowe, Aric Snee

The Selfie Arm was created from a fascination with the idea of technology and its illusionary "connectedness" and "sociability". It is a sarcastic solution to taking a mindlessly snap picture of oneself, and also a commentary on the growing selfie-stick phenomenon and the constant, gnawing need for social Internet validation. Made of fiberglass, it is lightweight and portable.

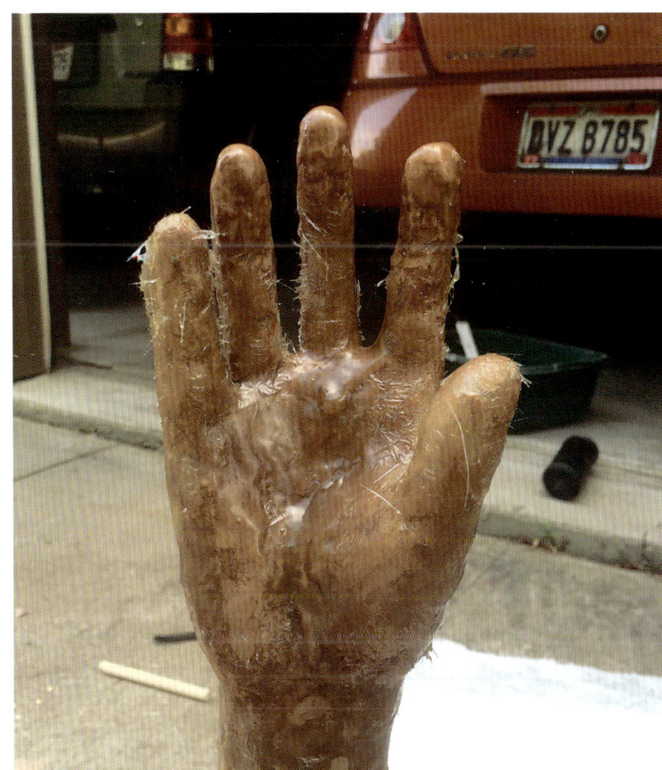

DVZ 8785

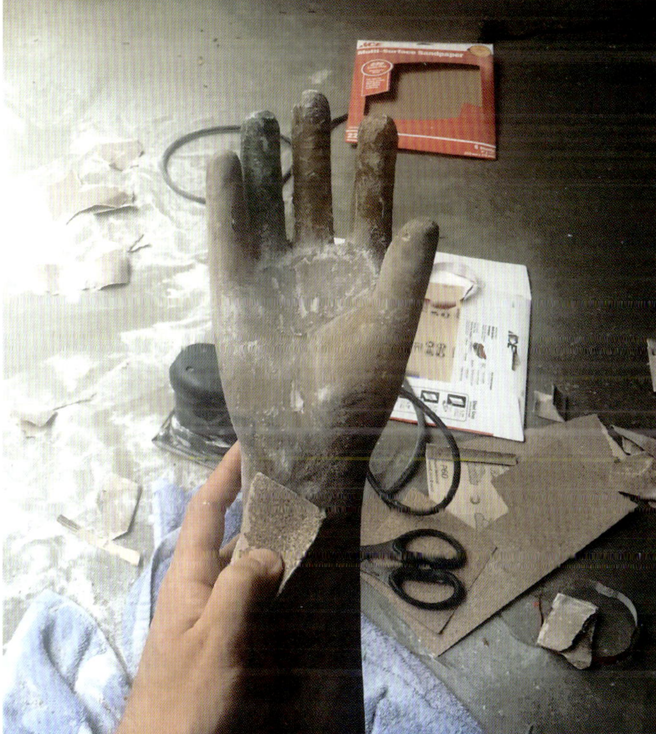

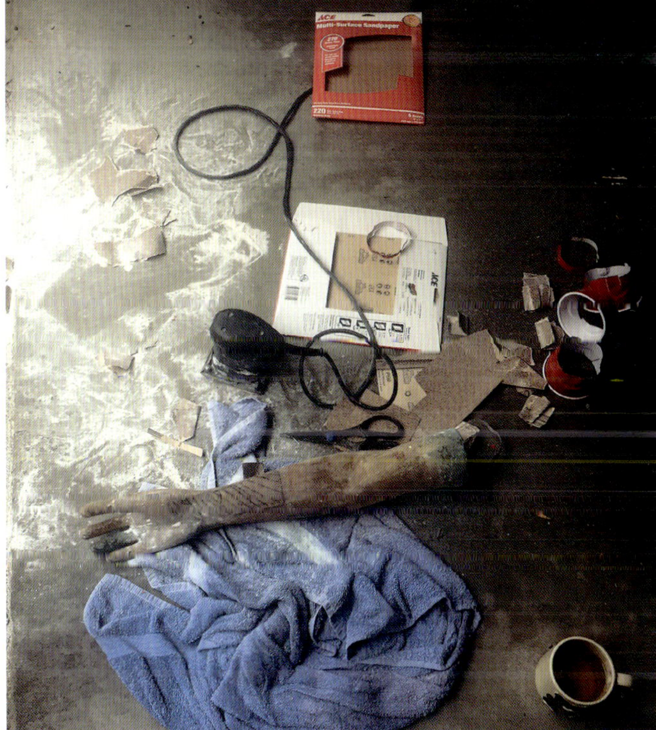

ACE
Multi-Surface Sandpaper

Texture

Materials are a crucial element in product design, functionally or aesthetically. The utilization and imitation of a natural texture has helped to improve the form, quality and even practical use of a product. Texture delivers a particular design idea and psychological experience. The following projects show how natural texture has been creatively employed in product design.

A Body of Skin

Designer Studio 9191

These chairs seek to explore the intricate subtleties of skin and flesh. A curious connection was established between the object and the user. Silicone was used as the basic material in the work because it is the closest texture to that of real skin and has an evocative visual impact. Human pheromones and aftershave were added to give a smell of skin.

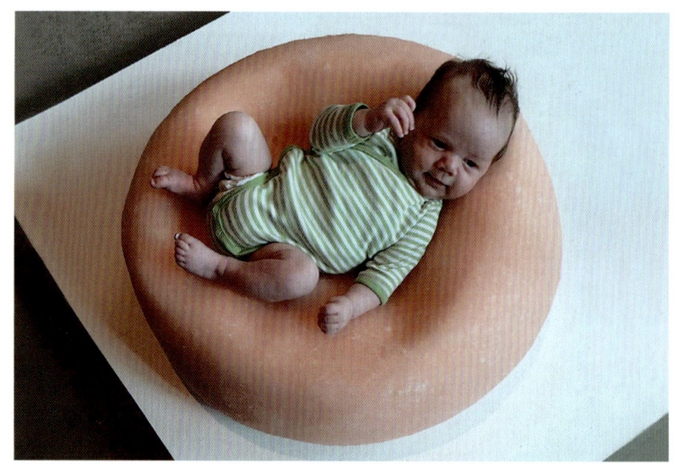

··· Interview with Studio 9191···

1. What did you take into account when it came to the choice of material and technique?

>>Informed by sculptural techniques and processes, the final material and technique choice was a natural combination of the design process, experimentation and resources. It is important in the design process to question and reconsider things, asking what they could be rather than what they are. In this way you can work in new contexts.

2. Is this product manufactured purely or partly by hand? Do you have a preference for hand-craft when you create?

>>This project was manufactured entirely by hand, as all my other projects are. Due to the nature of the work, it seemed only fitting that the human eye would better reinterpret the irregularities of human form and texture. It was quite a personal project for me and it was important for me to have that kind of relationship with my work. Humans and humanity are the motivation for my designs, and this is reflected in the work's handmade process.

3. What difficulties did you encounter during the production? Did you ever think that you should abandon your idea ?

>>Scale! I have a tendency to supersize everything and find it hard to return from this, but luckily sticking to human proportions acts as a guideline for this process.
I don't think I ever considered abandoning the work! Hurdles are part of the challenge and are essential to the process. The project evolved and developed with hurdles as well as hidden surprises.

4. What do you think about the prospect of a biomimetic product?

>>The human body is an amazing feat of nature, so it stands to reason that we would seek to replicate it, for all its properties. Skin is the largest organ of the body, which provides sensation, protects us and regulates our body temperature—everything that we take for granted in our daily life. The ability to replicate it or the function of other organs is one that is truly exciting and motivates designers and professionals in other areas.

Dematerialize Project

Designer Marcel Pasternak

The Dematerialize Project is a research project that aims to overcome computer-generated algorithms that create perfect forms and structures. Monotonous self-repeating patterns are easy to anticipate and therefore don't excite the human eye anymore. This is why Marcel Pasternak searched for unpredictable structures. He found them in nature. The study of fungi, roots and viruses helped him to overcome the learned compulsion to create regular patterns. The result is a "monster stool" formed of silicone-molded cauliflower.

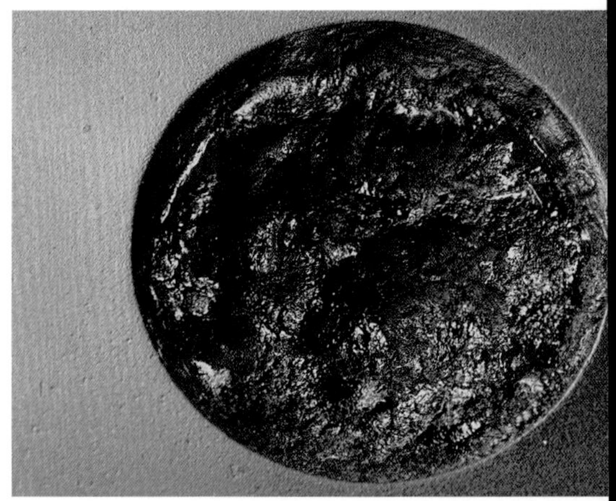

PASTERNAK

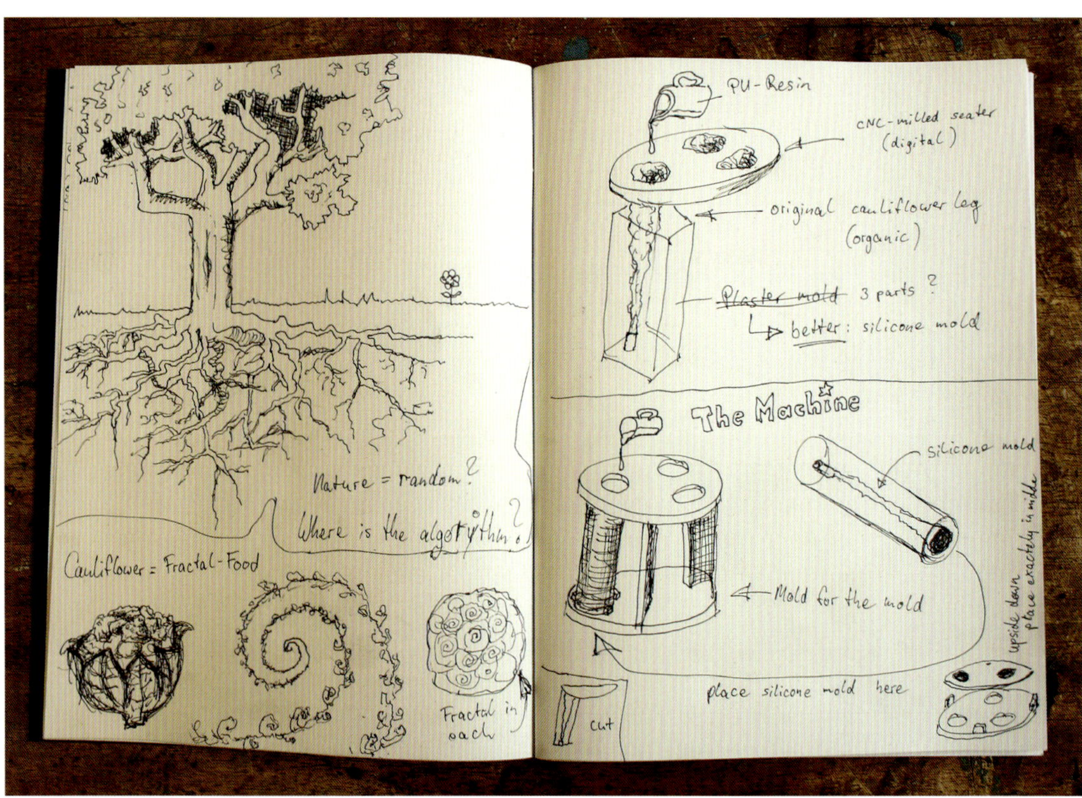

··· *Interview with Marcel Pasternak* ···

1. Is this design mass-produced or customizable?

>>This is a gallery production limited to 20 pieces.

2. Do you often take inspiration from nature?

>>Sure, I try to spend as much time as possible in nature. Nature is fantastic! It offers me inspiration as well as mental balance. I have realized that we can solve lots of problems by observing and analyzing nature. And this is exactly what I'm trying to communicate in my recent project bionicTOYS.

3. What do you think about the relation between biomimetics and product design? In your view, how does biomimetics influence a product functionally and aesthetically?

>>I am teaching biomimetics in schools at the moment. Children should learn how to be inspired by nature. Not by listening to my lecture inside the classroom, but by exploring nature outside in the woods. Meanwhile we do have good technology to get deeper insights into complex biological processes. But we are still too far away from understanding nature. In my opinion the first step is to get fascinated.

4. Does this final product meet your expectations? What do you think is most meaningful in this project?

>>My final product never meets my expectations. It's just one of a billion possibilities to present complex thoughts. And I feel that interactive installations are a much better medium to communicate those thoughts. The most meaningful aspect of this project is the almost dramatic appearance caused by contrasting two different worlds: the organic and the digital.

5. Is there an interesting story behind this cooperation that you would like to share with us?

>>I planned to use romanesco, a naturally fractal vegetable, for moulding instead of the cauliflower until a friend showed me an algorithm to imitate the fractal structure by code. This is why I couldn't use it to contrast with the perfect circle. Now I'm quite happy with the ugly, monster-like appearance.

Intertidal Deployment Objects

Studio Something Like This Design

Designer Trygve Faste, Jessica Swanson

The project is an exploration of the use of barnacles as an active participant in the completion of ceramic design work and of the marine environment as a collaborative partner in the generation of dynamic ceramic surfaces. This is a modular system of interchangeable forms that can be submerged into the ocean separately to encourage the growth of marine life. The final design of these pieces was informed by the technical constraints of barnacle growth and an aesthetic exploration of nautical hardware and other maritime equipment.

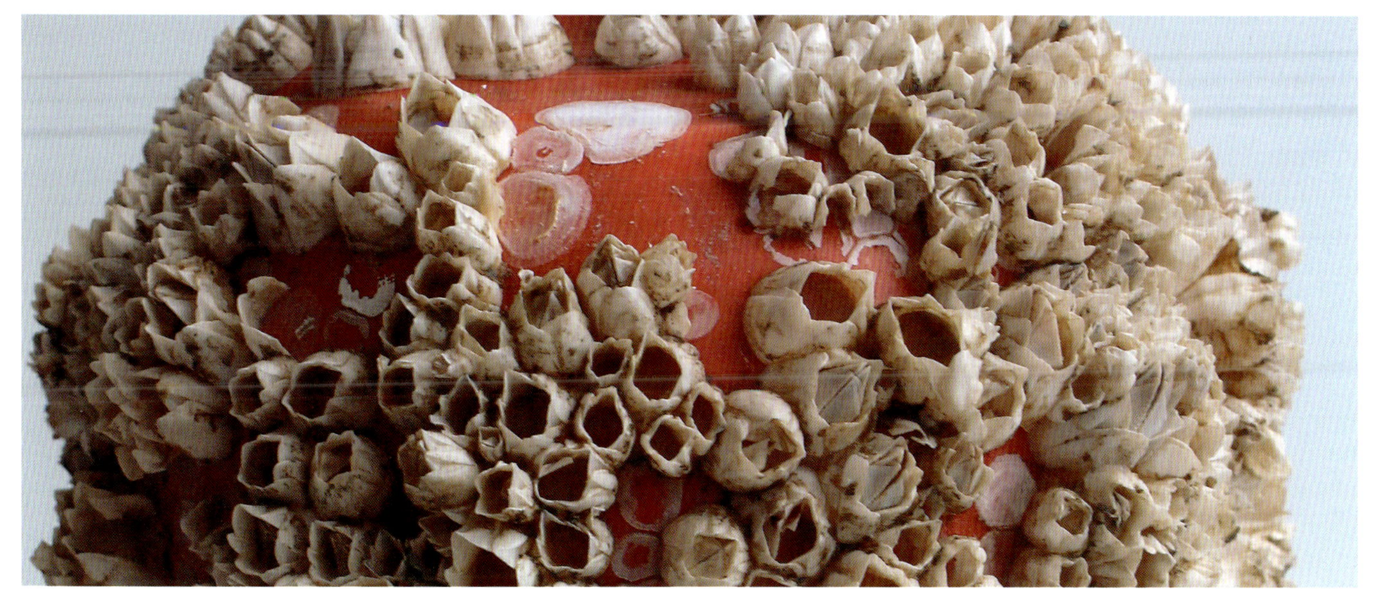

Texture

Energy Stool

Designer Marcel Pasternak

Inspired by artist Joseph Beuys' eco-cycle, Marcel Pasternak replaced modeling wax with real beeswax to increase the amount of energy in the lost wax casting process. The bronze seater of the casted stool glints in a golden honeycomb structure and pays tribute to the work of busy bees, offering users a resting place to restore their energy, giving it back to the insects.

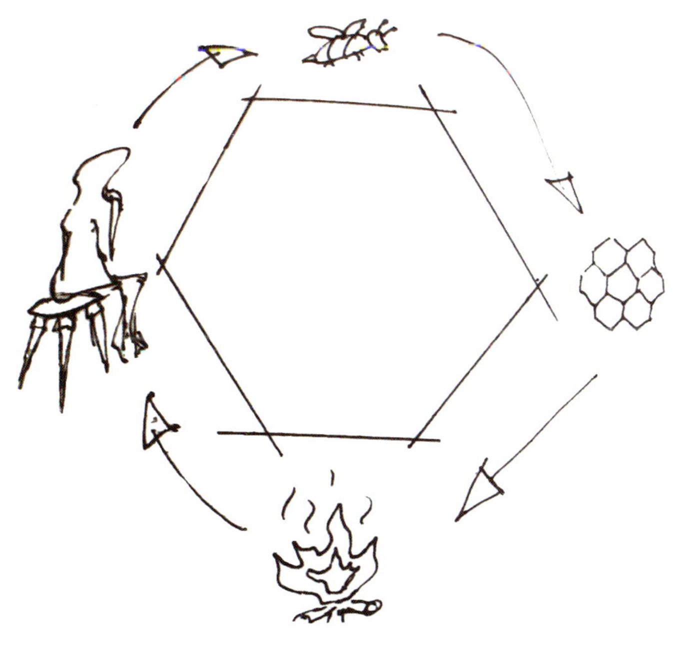

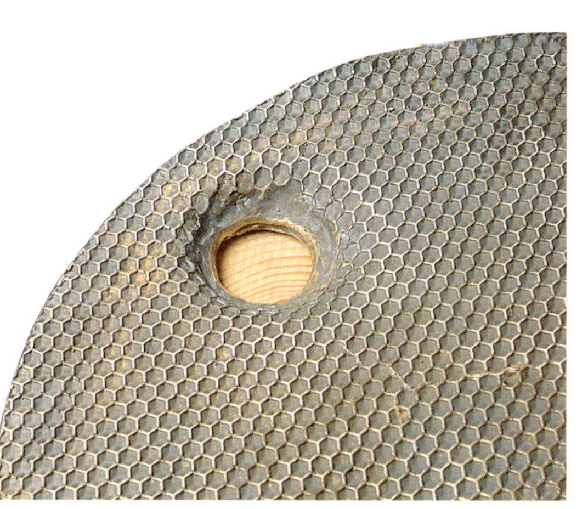

Lighting Cup

Studio NOTHING dESIGN GROUP

The Lighting Cup is made of translucent white ceramic clay. A classic oriental landscape painting is illustrated with translucency variation, which is done by designing the thickness of the cup, reproducing the shading characteristic of ink painting and delineating the mountains. It functions as a teacup and as a delicate lighting cover for the LED saucer.

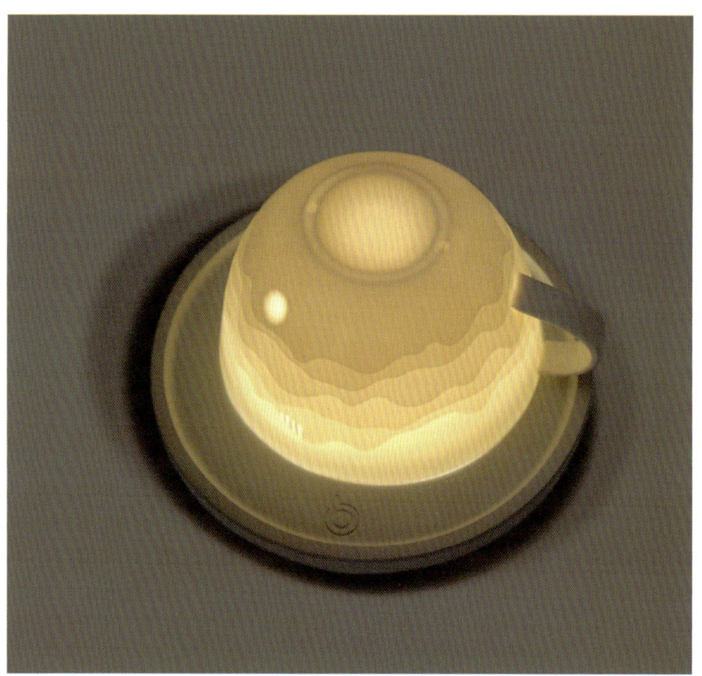

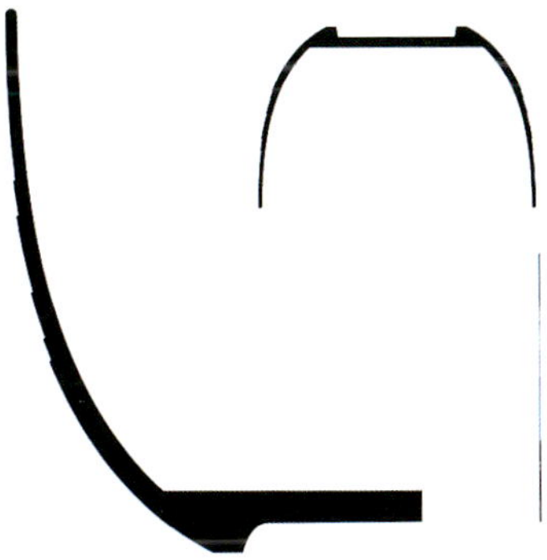

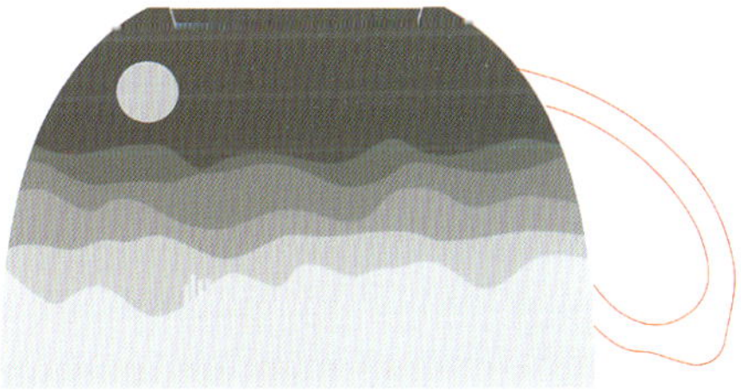

Marbled Stools

Designer Davide-Giulio Aquini

Marbled Stools are the result of research into materials and sustainability. The cushions on the plywood stools are made of recycled material polyurethane or polyethylene, which is usually used for acoustic insulation. This particular composition gives a hard, marbled look to the product, but its soft and comfortable nature delivers a surprising experience.

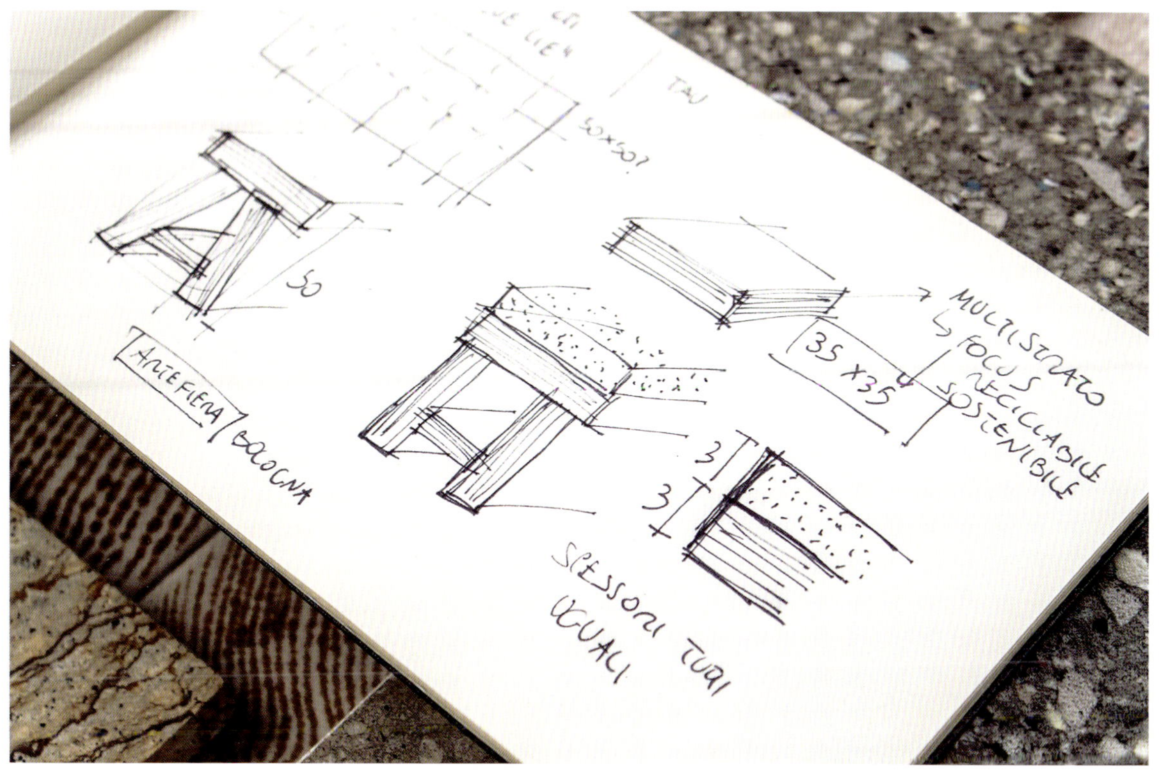
ARTEFIERA
BOLOGNA
50
MULTISTRATO
FOCUS
RICICLABILE
SOSTENIBILE
35 X 35
3
3
SPESSORI TUTTI
UGUALI

Stone Cushions

Studio Smarin

This design is a high-quality surrealistic set that functions practically as a floor cushion. The design is composed of over-sized pebbles and a resting area, with varying sizes and shapes that can be arranged according to the client's model, and is for contemporary interiors. The pebbles can be interpreted as a fanciful landscape of an ideal holiday or an enjoyable game.

Suface

Designer Daniel Chua

Surface is a music player with touch capabilities and also a work of art. It is a holistic exploration that combines complexity and simplicity. Irregular surfaces are drawn in a refined rectangle form, challenging how we perceive and define design aesthetics. Although marble is common in different industries, including for interiors and furniture, Surface was intended to push the boundary of the material itself through product design.

Roots

Designer Konstantin Kofta

This collection was intended to offer clarity of thoughts and space in the age of information overload to encourage people to go back to their roots and think deeply.

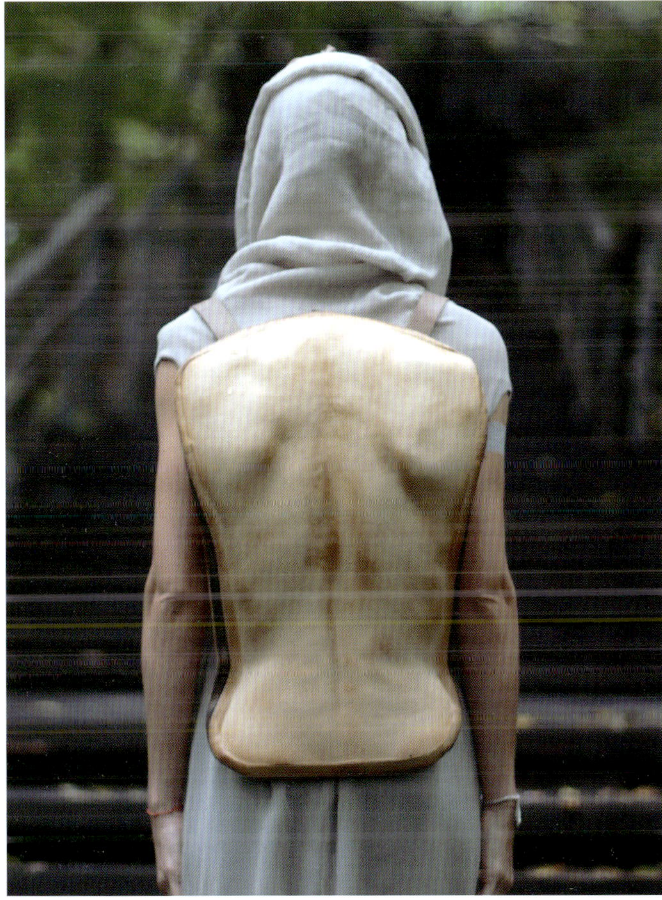

Pastizal Praxis

Designer Alexandra Kehayoglou

The pieces are produced with materials retrieved from the factory. The textile is weaved with hand tufting techniques, during which the artist manipulates a tufting gun on vertically framed rugs. The production process is long and complex because of the manual labor and technical precision required. The designer's work includes a catalog of memories of different native landscapes that she has visited, with the intention of preserving them in her own way.

Fruit Wares

Studio Mathery Studio

Fruit Wares is a handmade homewares collection inspired by fruit peels, including the Orange Jar, Avocado Vase, Banana Bowl, Rock Melon Coasters and Pineapple Punch Bowl. The vessels explore and reintroduce the natural textures of fruit, with each object produced in resin modeled on real fruit peels. Fruits were carefully selected and minutely cut into geometric shapes to be reassembled as product prototypes.

Diatom Helmet

Studio Paula Studio

Designer V. Ciampicacigli, S. Bartolucci

Inspired by the cellular structure of diatom, the goal was to increase the helmet's performance by reducing its weight and improving its durability. The helmet is formed of three layers of different materials (abs, d30, neoprene) joined together by ribs. The net pattern allows for perspiration and absorbs the impact of a crash.

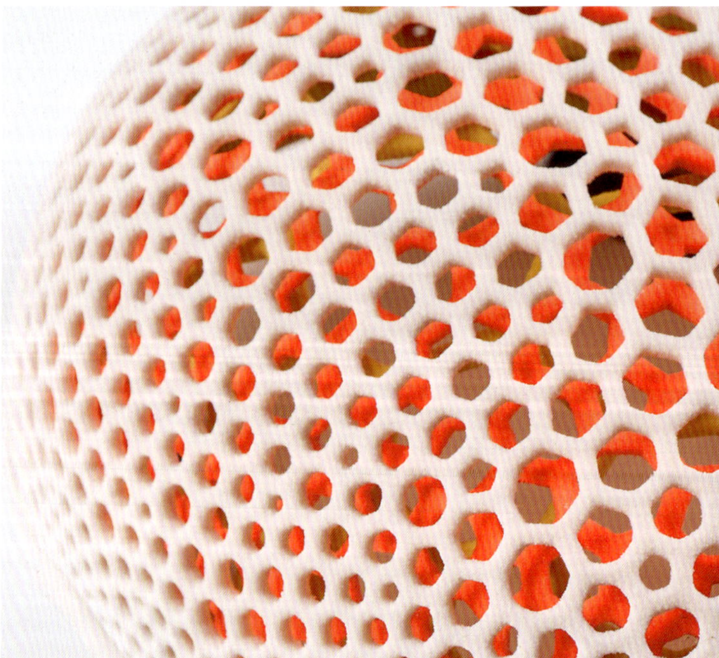

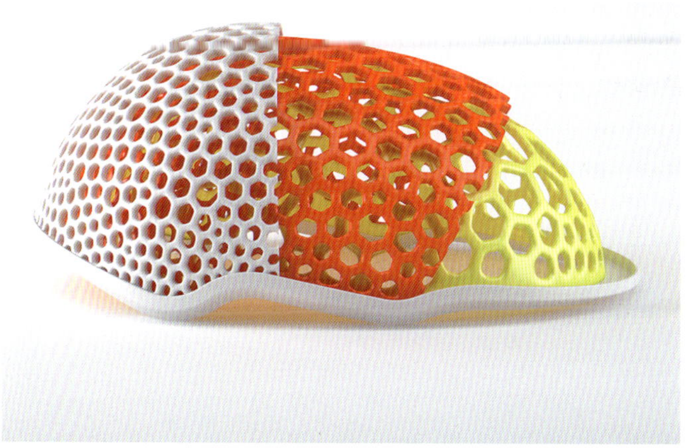

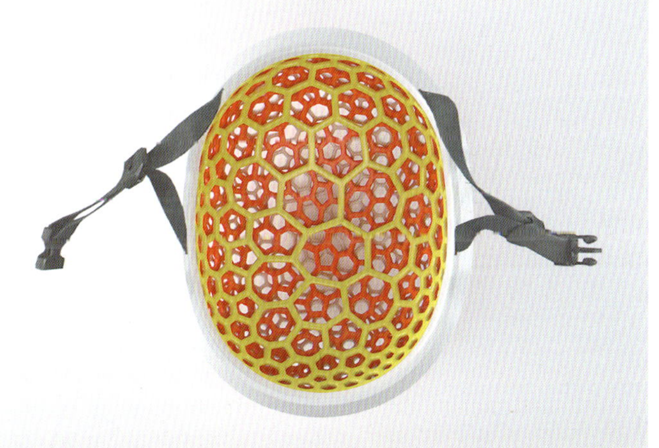

Liquid Glacial Table

Designer Zaha Hadid

The Liquid Glacial design embeds surface complexity and refraction within a powerful fluid dynamic. The elementary geometry of the flat table top appears transformed from static to fluid by the subtle waves and ripples evident below the surface, while the table's legs seem to pour from the horizontal in an intense vortex of water frozen in time. The transparent acrylic material amplifies this perception, adding depth and complexity through a flawless display of infinite kaleidoscopic refractions.

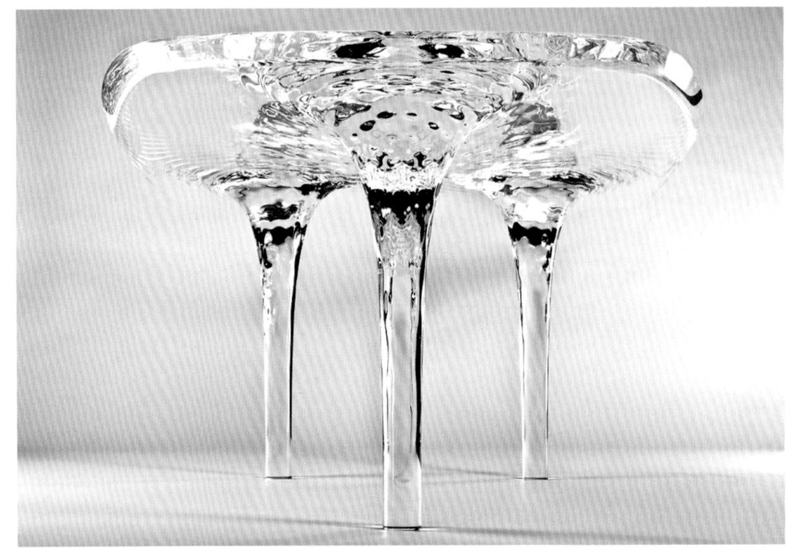

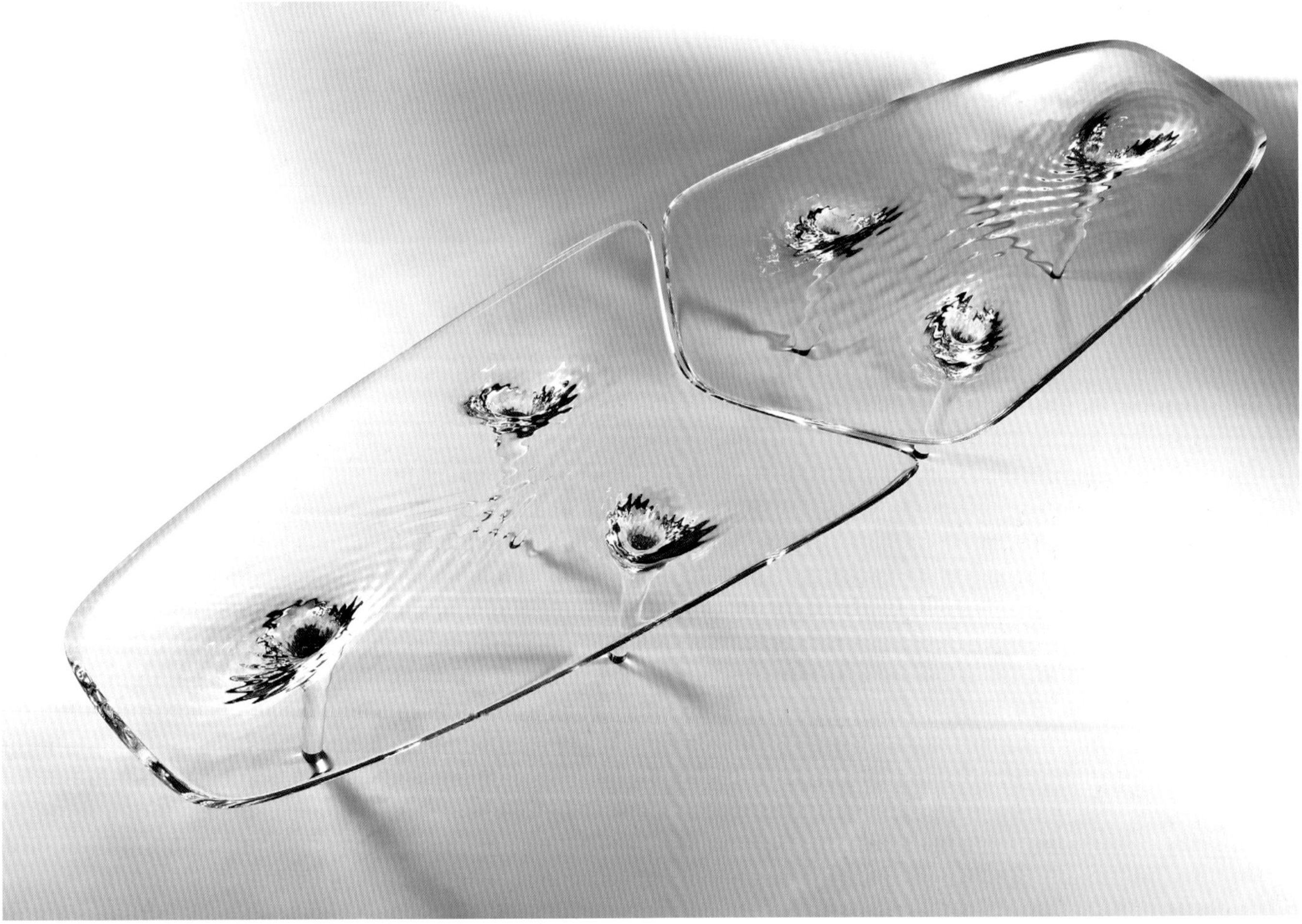

Reversed Volumes

Studio mischer'traxler

Reversed Volumes is a collection of bowls and plates shaped by attempts to capture the imprints of fruits, vegetables and leaves. The space between the bowl and the objects is filled with casting material. Once dried, the filling material adopts the shape of the container and the natural elements are reproduced to the finest detail. These imprints are then replicated in food-safe and waterproof resin, hand-crafted in a semi-industrial process which allows slight color variations.

Confluence

Designer Artonomos

Confluence is a small wooden tea tray carved out of birch plywood. The layers of the laminated ply accentuate the undulating form which emerges from the alternating dark and light seams. Niches and plateaus are carved to accommodate up to six small tea cups. A large central reservoir is formed by the landscape, where excessive tea naturally gathers to form a miniature lake.

Sponge

Studio Pott

Designer Miguel Ángel García Belmonte

The Sponge lamp comes as a prelude to the Sponge series and defines the basis of the brand's distinctive signature: applying traditional pottery techniques and natural materials to contemporary design. The lamp is a unique hand-crafted lighting element that is available in three different sizes, adding nature-inspired shapes and earth-toned colors to modern design. A soft and warm glow slips through the porous surface of each sphere, creating a unique and serene atmosphere.

SpongeUp!

Studio Pott

Designer Miguel Ángel García Belmonte

The SpongeUp! ceramic pendant light is a natural evolution of the Sponge lamps trilogy, not only by adding new sizes and new colors to its predecessor, but also by literally taking it to a new level.
It retains the traditional handmade techniques and combines them with contemporary lighting arrangements. When the light is turned on, the sponge-like surface of the lamp creates a unique and soft stellar ambiance in the room. When turned off, the lamp becomes an organic decorative element with its mat surface and earth-toned colors.

SpongeOh!

Studio Pott

Designer Miguel Ángel García Belmonte

The Sponge lamps trilogy concludes with the SpongeOh! series, a hand-crafted ceramic light collection which has shapes and textures as its protagonists. Hand-made in Totana in southern Spain, these pendant lights propose a balanced juxtaposition of typical smooth pottery and the distinctive porous element of sponge, which generates a uniquely textured lighting atmosphere. The lamp is available in 30 cm and 36 cm sizes, with two color choices: soft terracotta and white.

Stripped

Designer Floris Wubben

To maintain the natural form of a tree branch as much as possible, Stripped is made out of only one branch, which is split into three parts to act as the lamp's legs. The bark is almost entirely pealed from the branch and with a rotating movement formed into a lamp shade. Each part of the tree branch gains a new function without losing its natural and exceptional appearance.

Moonlight

Designer Marjan van Aubel

Moon Light is made out of self-developed foam porcelain, a kind of lightweight porcelain that expands in the kiln up to 300% in size. The design explores the material's aesthetic properties, making use of its translucency to diffuse light, which glows gently through a foam porcelain disk, whose cratered surface is reminiscent of the lunar landscape.

Myx Project

Designer Jonas Edvard

The project involves a new material and a new production method: it is a development of a mushroom mycelium textile and a lamp in the same material. The material consists of an oyster mushroom organism, recycled from a commercial mushroom production plant, and hemp fibers, which are left to mix together for 2 to 3 weeks before a soft living textile is formed. It takes another 2 to 3 weeks for the textile to be molded into a lamp or other products with the harvesting of the healthy and nutritious fungi. The lamp is afterwards dehydrated to become a lightweight and strong functional object which is biodegradable and flameproof.

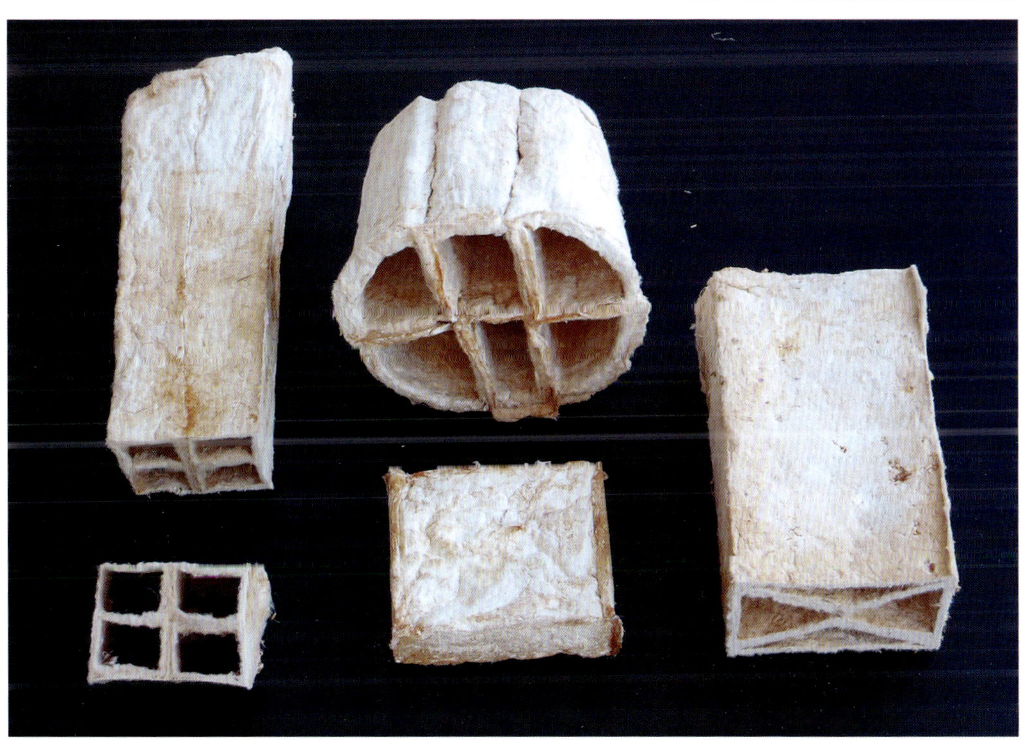

Terroir Project

Designer Jonas Edvard, Nikolaj Steenfatt

This Project includes a chair and a lamp made from a strong material of brown algea and recycled paper. The material consists of the seaweed collected along the shore of Denmark. The brown algae contain high amounts of natural alginate, which stabilizes the material and gives it a dark brown color. Marine algae grow all over the world and are edible; they are usually used as a fertilizer or as a stabilizer in food. Besides being a renewable resource, the seaweed products can be 100% recycled or decomposed and used as a fertilizer for new life.

Marine Light

Designer Nir Meiri

This is a project inspired by the sea. Through the unconventional use of seaweed as a main material for a domestic environment, the product plays on the tension between the artistic and the commercial. The lamp consists of a metal base and a structure of thin metal strings that function as the lamp shade. The seaweed is placed on metal strings while it is still fresh. As it dries, it shrinks and obtains the form of the lamp shade. A mixture of preserving material is used. The light reflected through the seaweed and the form of the lamp are intended to induce underwater feelings.

Graft

Designer Qiyun Deng

Graft is a series of disposable tableware made of bioplastic PLA that reveals its source materials—plants. Texture and form in nature autonomously exist with a function that can be utilized for another purpose. A celery stem could serve as the handle of a fork; a petal of artichoke could become the bowl of spoon. Graft's extraordinary visual and haptic sensation would make you hesitate to throw it away.

Stone Foam Stool

Designer Matthijs Kok

This is a stool with a hard look that is unexpectedly soft. After researching polyurethane material, the designer developed a recipe for stone foam. A custom-made silicone mold is filled with the liquid stone foam mixture. The mixture increases sixteen times in volume, during which process the stone foam takes the shape of the mold. The clay granules are soaked in the casting and the stone texture appears. The casting is fine-tuned with multiple gray shades for a more natural effect, while the addition of clay grain and pigment to the liquid foam gives a raw texture.

Basalt

Studio Normal Studio

This collection of five scorched wooden coffee tables is created from a single oak trunk, which has been cut and reassembled to retain only the rings formed by the heartwood, the highest quality timber. Each piece is hand-carved and scorched using a blowtorch. The finishing process gives a mineral dimension to the wood, subtly revealing its nature.

Stone Chair

Studio Jishnuram C. A.

This is a project designed for a Stone-Age-themed restaurant. Taking inspiration from the Stone Age—caves and stone tools—the chair is suitable for gardens and other open-space areas. It is made out of an iron seat skeleton and cement. Black oxide is used to enhance its rock-like appearance.

Lentill

Studio Monomoka

Designer Katarzyna Gwiazdowska, Monika Gwiazdowska

The seat consists of 186 lentil-like elements crocheted out of natural cotton cord, fixed on a cross-legs wooden base with two metal rings.

The Hive

Studio Monomoka

Designer Katarzyna Gwiazdowska, Monika Gwiazdowska

This sofa is made of over 1600 pale gray crocheted linen modules, the result of months of intensive hand work. The combination of traditional crocheting techniques and modern form has made each piece unique.

Mer Noire—Cliff Edition

Designer Damien Gernay

This series of tables is an attempt to capture a moment of nature and transform it into a daily element of our lives. To realize the image in mind, a new technique called embossed leather was developed. The production process includes 3D modeling for the leather mold and the use of an expanding resin to emboss the leather.

Cuckoo X CLOCK—Tree

Studio haoshi

Designer Griffin Yang

In contrast to a traditional cuckoo clock, this one comes with one bird in the clock and another mounted outside on the wall. Every hour the bird in the tree comes out to meet its friend and sing a birdsong. The sound mechanism has been arranged to start the first birdsong at six in the morning and the last at ten in the evening.

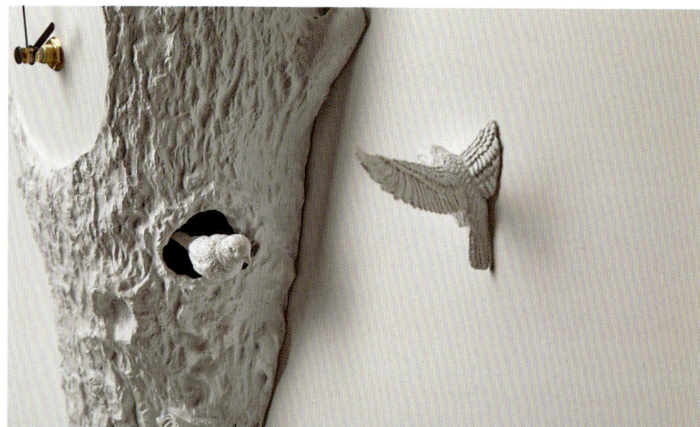

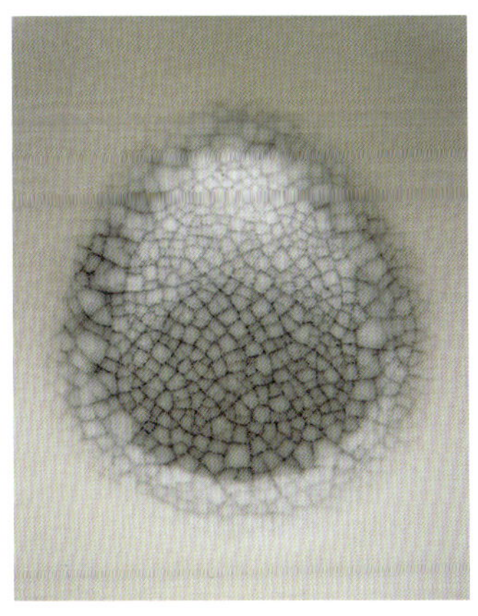

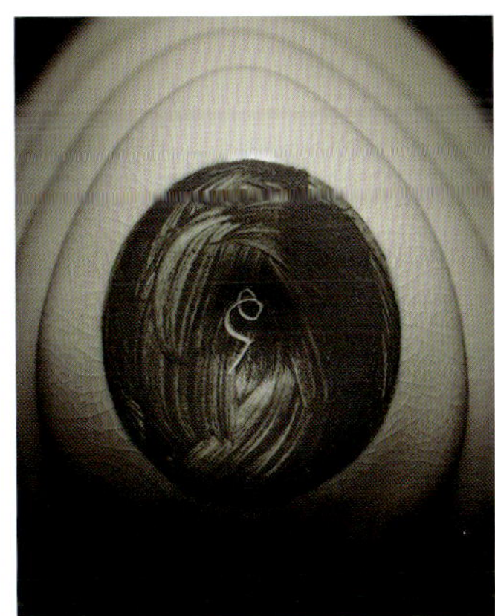

Shiro-Satsuma cs003

Studio nendo

This particular four-bowl set is made of shirosatsuma, a type of Satsuma-yaki ceramic ware. An enamel glaze has been applied to the white background so that it resembles the color and shape of an egg. The entire piece demonstrates the effect of kannyu, a method whereby cracks are intentionally formed due to a difference of contraction rate between the ceramic and the enamel. Pigmented ink is then poured onto the cracks from inside the container and pushed through with different concentrations of color, creating gradated hints of black oozing through the basic white surface.

Propolis Vessels

Designer Marlène Huissoud

Already science is exploring insects' potential for food production and for satisfying our future dietary needs, but the designer is primarily interested in using insects as co-partners in the design process, not in consuming them. This collection of engraved vessels is a combination of self-developed glass techniques and propolis, a natural bio-degradable resin produced by honey bees. The black color of the propolis results from the use of rubber trees as the plant source.

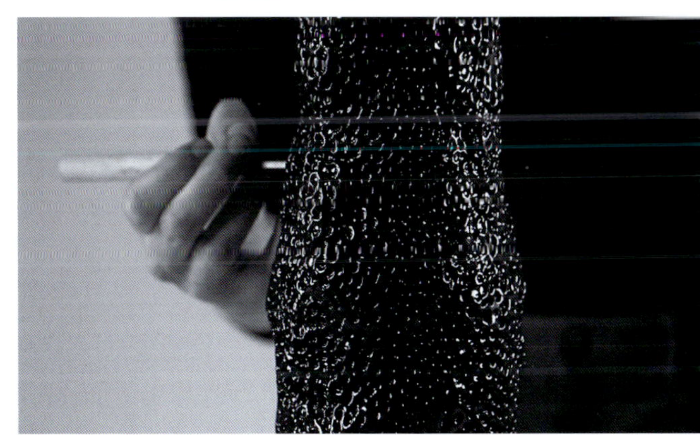

Texture

Wooden Leather

Designer Marlène Huissoud

The fibers in silkworm cocoon contain a natural glue called Sericin, which is a resinous substance that links the silk fibers together in the raw stage of the sericulture. Sericin can be activated by spraying water and heating the fibers. The outcome of this process is a kind of strong paper. To give strength to this material and change its natural state, black propolis was applied onto the paper. The result is a wooden leathered material, which has been used to create products such as cabinet, light and rug.

Idream

Designer Martín Azúa

This iPhone-like dispenser, with a small hole holding sandalwood oil, proposes a disconnection ritual. Placed among the sheets or under the pillow, it helps the user to relieve stress and fall asleep. The ripples on the surface are a visualization of the user's thoughts dissolving in the sandalwood oil as he or she sleeps.

The Tread Carpet

Designer Martín Azúa

The footprints carpet is made of esparto grass, a very common plant in Mediterranean areas with which espadrilles soles and rugs are traditionally made. Esparto is a 100% natural material with a particular texture that transmits a typical Mediterranean feel. It is customizable in several measures and shapes.

Di Corte

Studio Resign

Designer Andrea Magnani, Giovanni Delvecchio, Elisabetta Amatori

This project restored these wood chairs to their original coats of finish—bark. The bark was gathered and selected by typology and glued to the chair one piece at a time, imitating the textures that are characteristic of trees.

The adoption of a functional system in nature is considered to be the highest level of organic product design. Function-oriented organic design takes inspiration from the outstanding characteristics of existing natural systems and mimics them technically to create more beneficial products for human life. Designers have been trying to produce better designed, more beautiful and more functional products while improving their own design thinking and skills.

Setu Chair

Studio Studio 7.5

The Setu chair is characterized by a pair of flexible beams that span a pliable membrane, thus creating the right combination of support adaptivity. By introducing a two-component polymer material to a classical membrane chair construction, the side trusses become a dynamic kinematic structure that automatically adapts to different body sizes. This highly integrated design and its gentle bending in use recall motions found in nature. As a result, plastic, which was formerly seen as artificial and used as a surrogate for "real" materials, gains unique value and recognition.

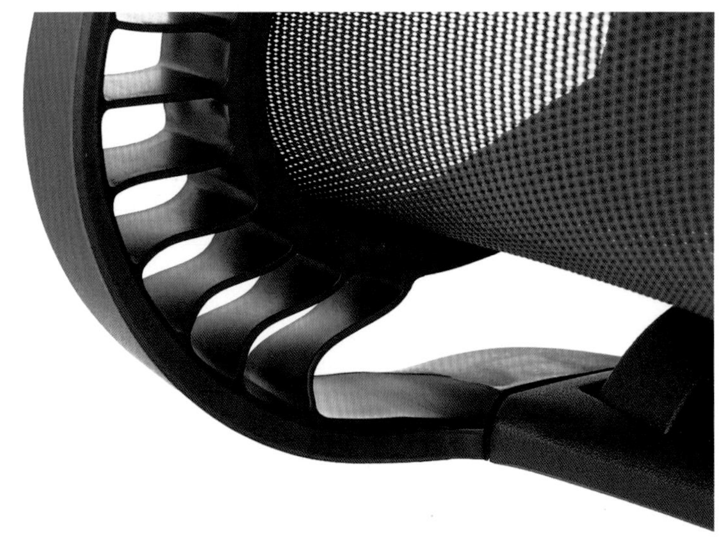

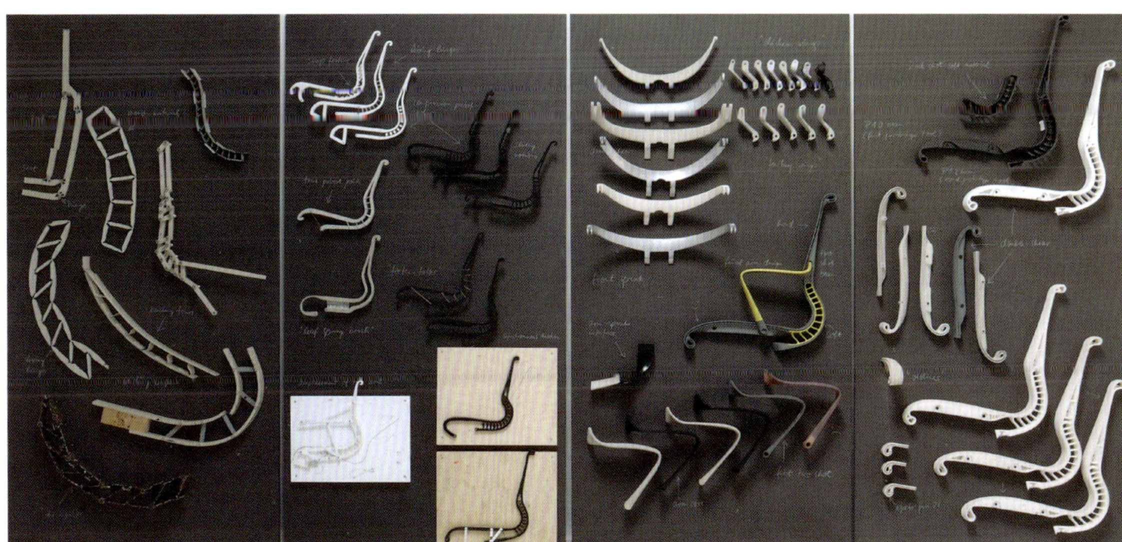

… Interview with Studio 7.5 …

1. What do you think one should take into account for a good chair design?

>>Firstly, a chair is an object that conveys cultural and aesthetic values in a particular way; almost every architect and designer feels the need to creatively express themselves by designing a chair. Secondly, a chair is a tool for people to forget gravity for a while and focus on something else. Back pain has become a big health issue in modern society as many professions spend their time sitting in front of computers for long periods. In our eyes designing a chair is by no means designing a static object, but rather a tool that allows for a dynamic change of postures to support a sitter's health.

2. We could find in this project your reflection on ergonomics and biomimetics. What do you think about biomimetic design?

>>We don't think that there is big gap between the building principles of the man-made environment and nature. One could argue that both systems need to withstand gravity and other laws of physics that define structural necessities in order to function. So if our product looks biomimetic it is not so much a result of imitating nature but of listening to the laws of physics, with our ambition to make construction pliable to the human body and to reduce the amount of material without losing structural integrity. Trying to create lightweight objects means striving for elegant constructions, and that's not only an environmental concern. Reducing weight usually also makes it easier for people to interact with these objects.

3. What do we need to consider when it comes to the choice of material during production?

>>We think that we can solve many material challenges by using the power of geometry, for example you can dial in the material stiffness by modulating the geometry. This is also helpful when choosing a material as many materials come in different variants like foam, fibers and solids, which can be combined according to the structural needs of your product and are recyclable as one material. So we strive to use only common materials that are recyclable and as few of them as possible, assembled in such a way that they can be disassembled as well.

Rostrum

Designer Bojan Kanlic

The essential idea for this project is based on biomimetics—the application of biological methods and systems found in nature to modern technology and design. The way that birds eat smartly with their beaks interested the designer immensely, and brought up this new idea in cutlery design which combines all the necessary functions for eating.

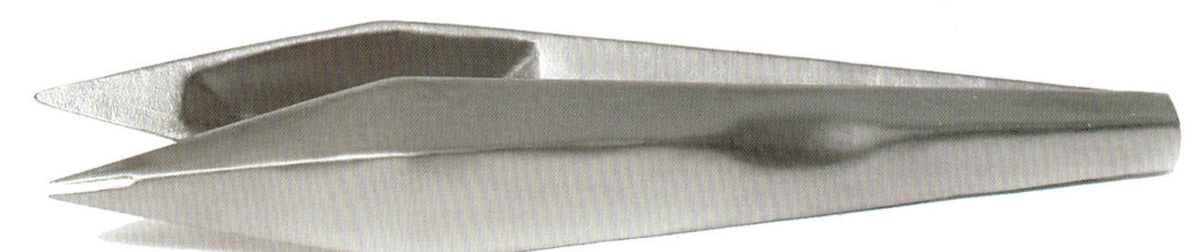

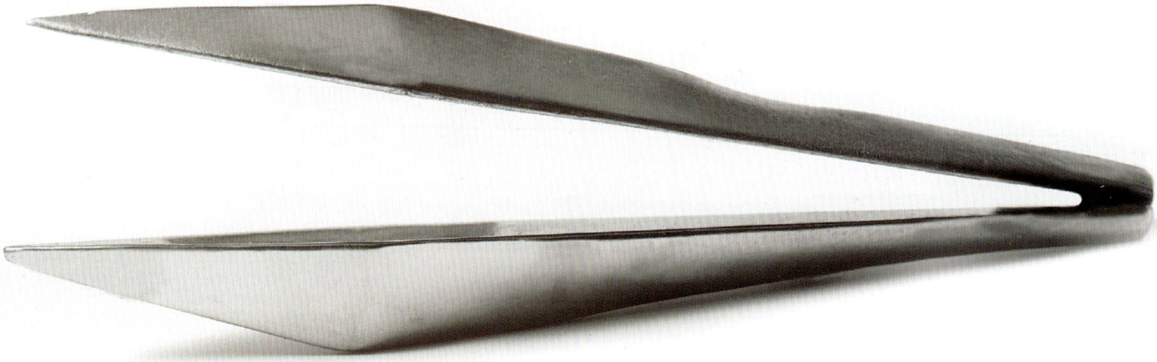

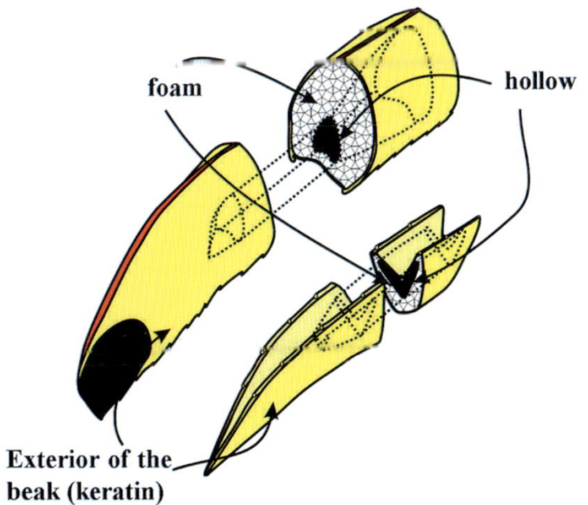

··· Interview with Bojan Kanlic ···

1. What's your view of the fact that people tend to value much more the combination of function and aesthetics?

>>Aesthetics is sort of emotional function, indispensable to a good design. From history we learn that products which aspired to be just functional or just aesthetic usually in the end did not fulfill even these particular aspects. There is nothing wrong with design being beautiful and functional.

2. What do you think about biomimetic design?

>>I think we've come to the point in design where innovation is becoming inaccessible if we continue with traditional approaches, materials and systems. In spite of new technological developments, biomimetics is one of the most inspiring fields of research. Elements, models and systems from nature are applicable to all aspects of design and certainly can improve all aspects of life, so I think biomimetics is definitely the future of design.

3. What do you take into consideration when you create or recreate a product?

>>The design process is complex and there are many things that you have to take into consideration, but for me it is always important that there is a strong idea behind it, a concept or a message that will make people think. A design should not only be functional but should also try to change people's ideas and influence society. We are surrounded by different designs and they define the way we live. So designers should take advantage of this potential to give a quality life to society, and should not just create products for their own purposes.

Link

Designer Christian Sjöström

Inspired by molecular structure and repeated elements, this system of three flexibly connected parts makes it possible for the users to create their own furniture. The round wooden parts combined with ball joints allow this dynamic expression, while the combination of ash wood and anodized aluminum gives the functional product a unique appearance.

··· Interview with Christian Sjöström ···

1. What's your view of the fact that people tend to value much more the combination of function and aesthetics?

>>It seems natural to desire both. When using a product it's easy to tell whether it was given the thought and sensitivity required to make it both functional and aesthetic. Though I think sometimes defining function is difficult and aesthetics tends to be subjective.
I see a lot of beautiful objects that don't fulfill their most basic functions, like a teapot that leaks water down its body while pouring out the tea. A product should evoke good feelings; this is why it is important to find a balance of functional and aesthetic attributes.

2. What do you think about biomimetic design?

>>Looking to living things for reference is good. It can lead to interesting aesthetic results and when deeply understood it can be used to solve our daily problems. Some architects and designers are working almost solely within this realm of design, for example, to create better environments that adapt to humidity and light or absorb water from the air like a beetle.

3. What do you take into consideration when you create or recreate a product?

>>As a designer I believe I have a responsibility to develop products with respect for man and nature. With a focus on function, sustainability and usability throughout the design process, I do my best to create good and long-lasting products. For me it's important that what I develop either solves a problem or makes life easier in some way. The design process for every product can be very different, but in every project I keep a curious and open mind—asking lots of questions, studying behaviors, experimenting and investigating techniques and materials.

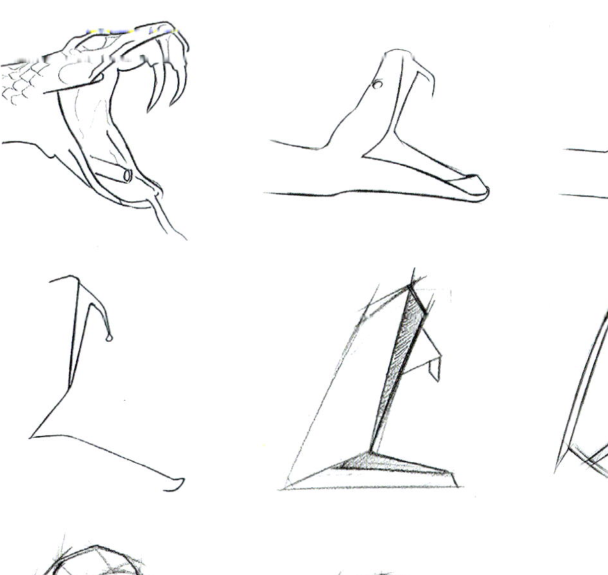

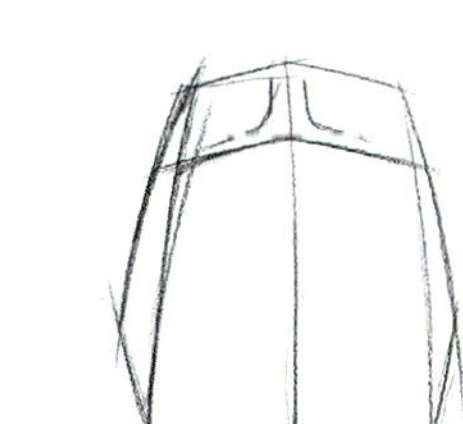

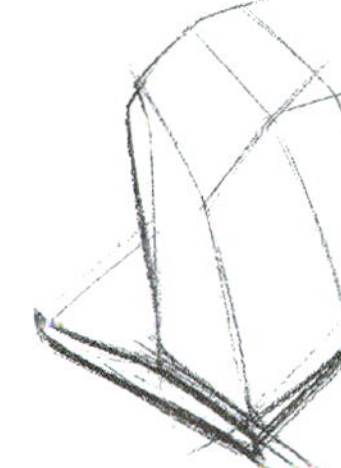

Coffee Maker

Designer Mukesh Kumar

To achieve a humorous connection between coffee and venom, the organic shape of a rattlesnake has been studied and used to create a new type of coffee maker. The logo mark was derived from the same motif, the scale of the snake.

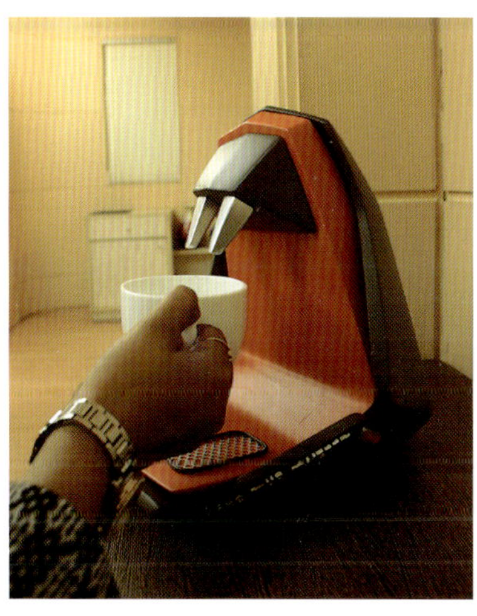

Cirrata

Designer Markus Johansson

The Cirrata glows in the darkness of the human living space in the way that jellyfish light up the sea. It is one of the series of lamps that explores the possibility of the material Corian.

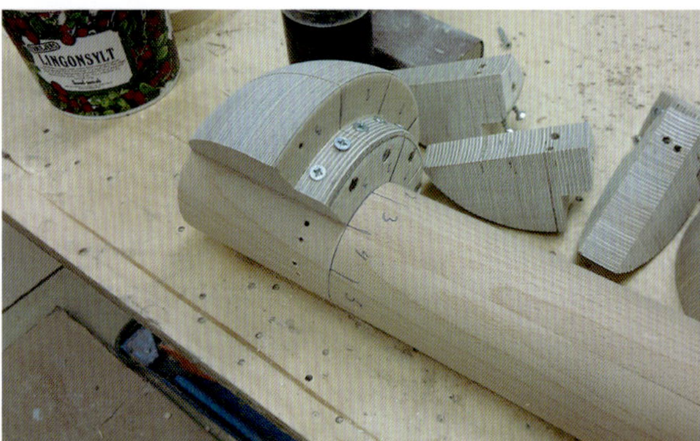

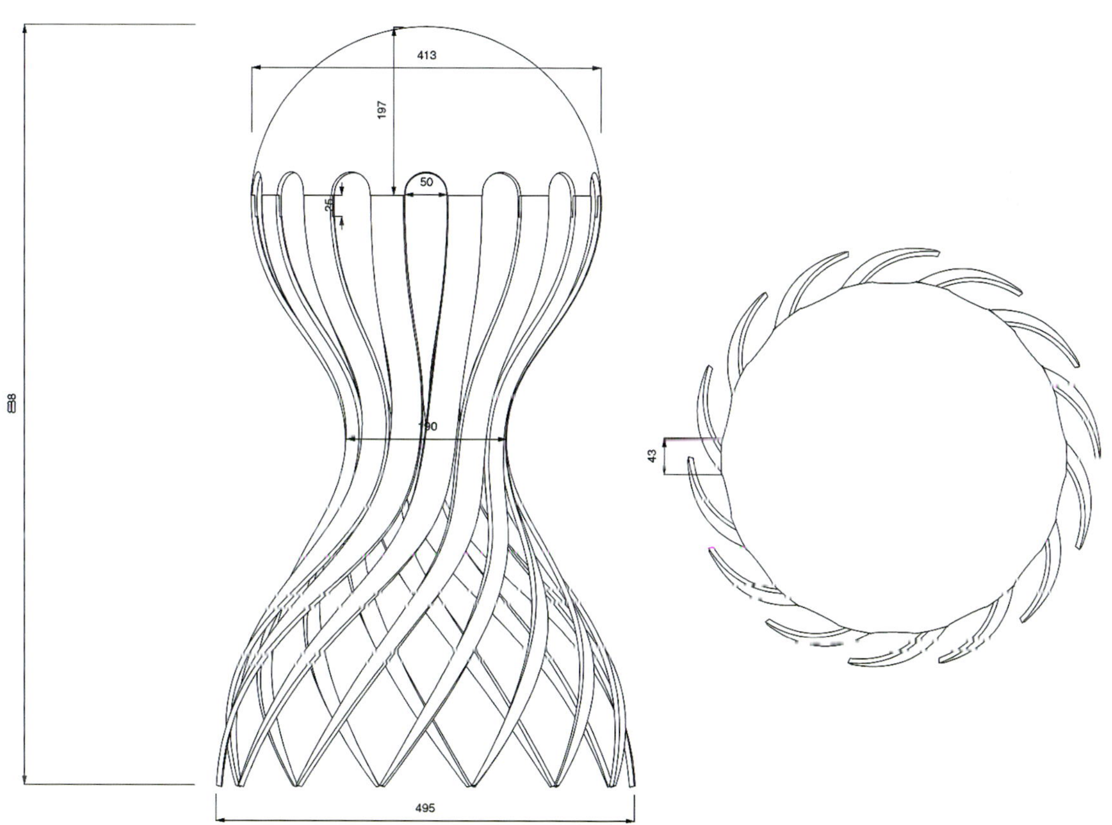
413
197
50
25
190
43
495

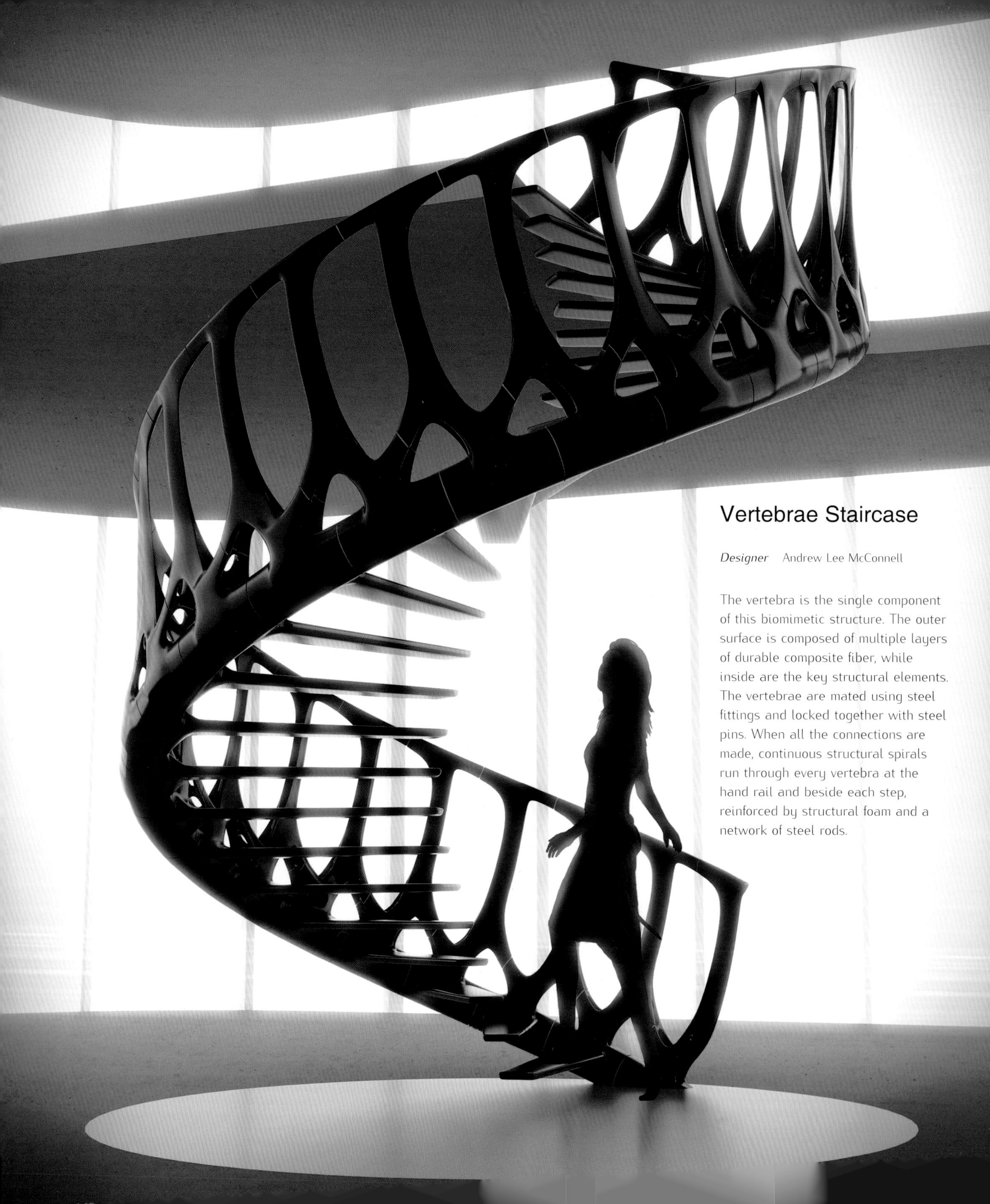

Vertebrae Staircase

Designer Andrew Lee McConnell

The vertebra is the single component of this biomimetic structure. The outer surface is composed of multiple layers of durable composite fiber, while inside are the key structural elements. The vertebrae are mated using steel fittings and locked together with steel pins. When all the connections are made, continuous structural spirals run through every vertebra at the hand rail and beside each step, reinforced by structural foam and a network of steel rods.

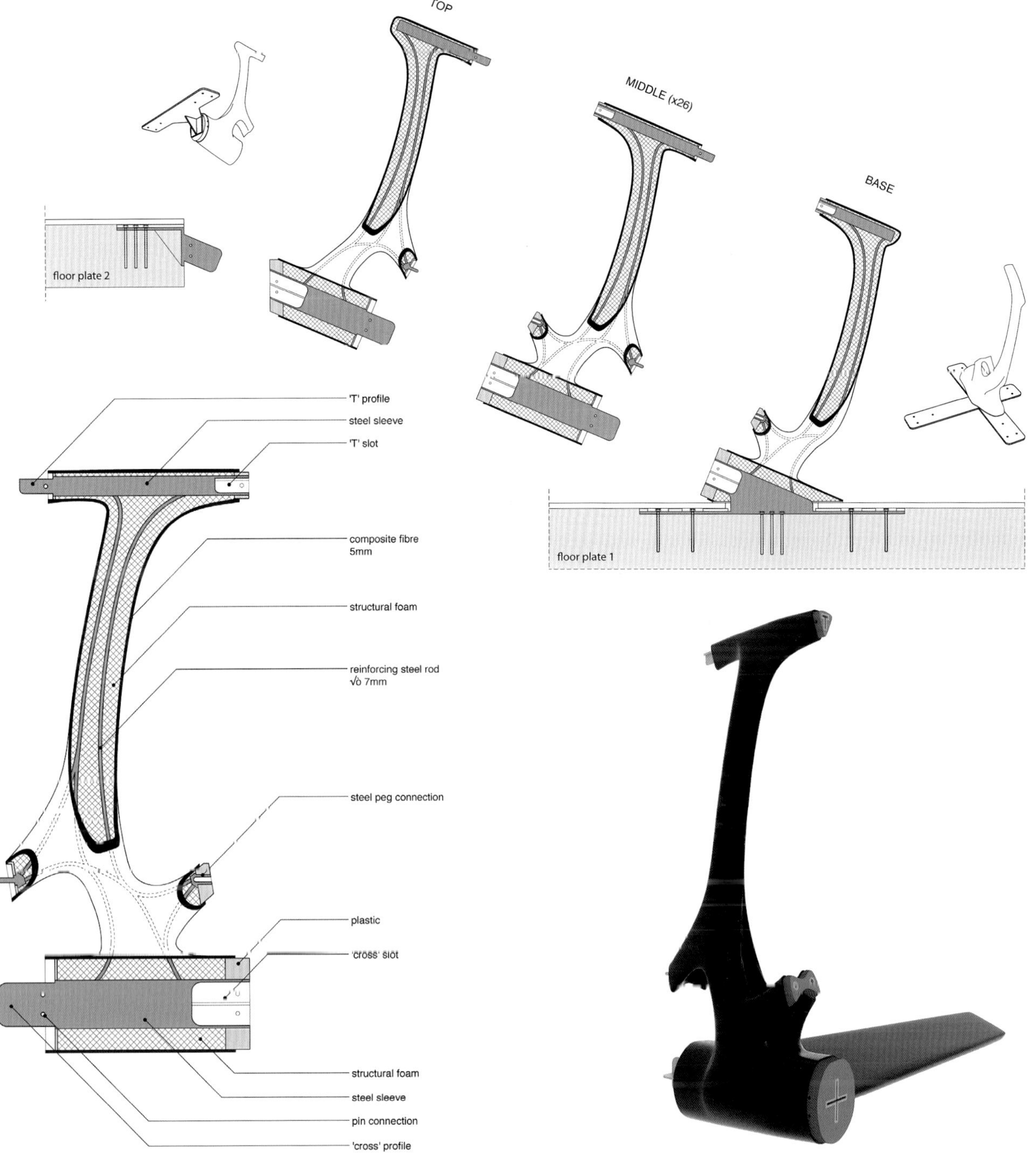
TOP
MIDDLE (x26)
BASE
floor plate 2
floor plate 1
'T' profile
steel sleeve
'T' slot
composite fibre
5mm
structural foam
reinforcing steel rod
√ò 7mm
steel peg connection
plastic
'cross' slot
structural foam
steel sleeve
pin connection
'cross' profile

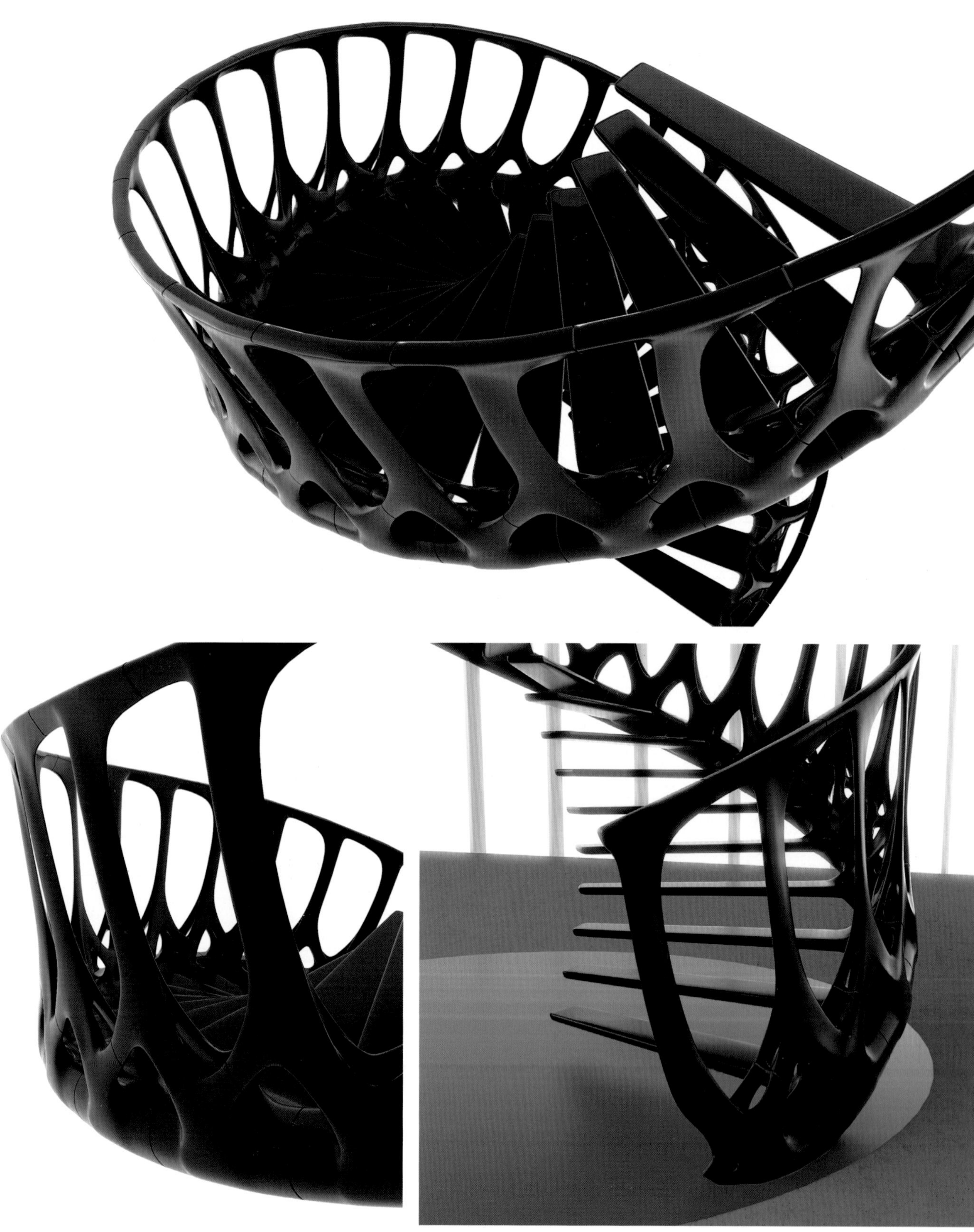

The Cosmos Bed

Designer Natalia Rumyantseva

This space-capsule-like bed, with glittering stars adding a feeling of flight, helps users to relax and fall asleep more easily, working on four human senses: sight, smell, sound and touch. There are built-in speakers, fragrance dispensers and LEDs, giving a therapeutic effect. The comfortable mattress equipped with a special tilt mechanism can be adjusted to meet different needs.

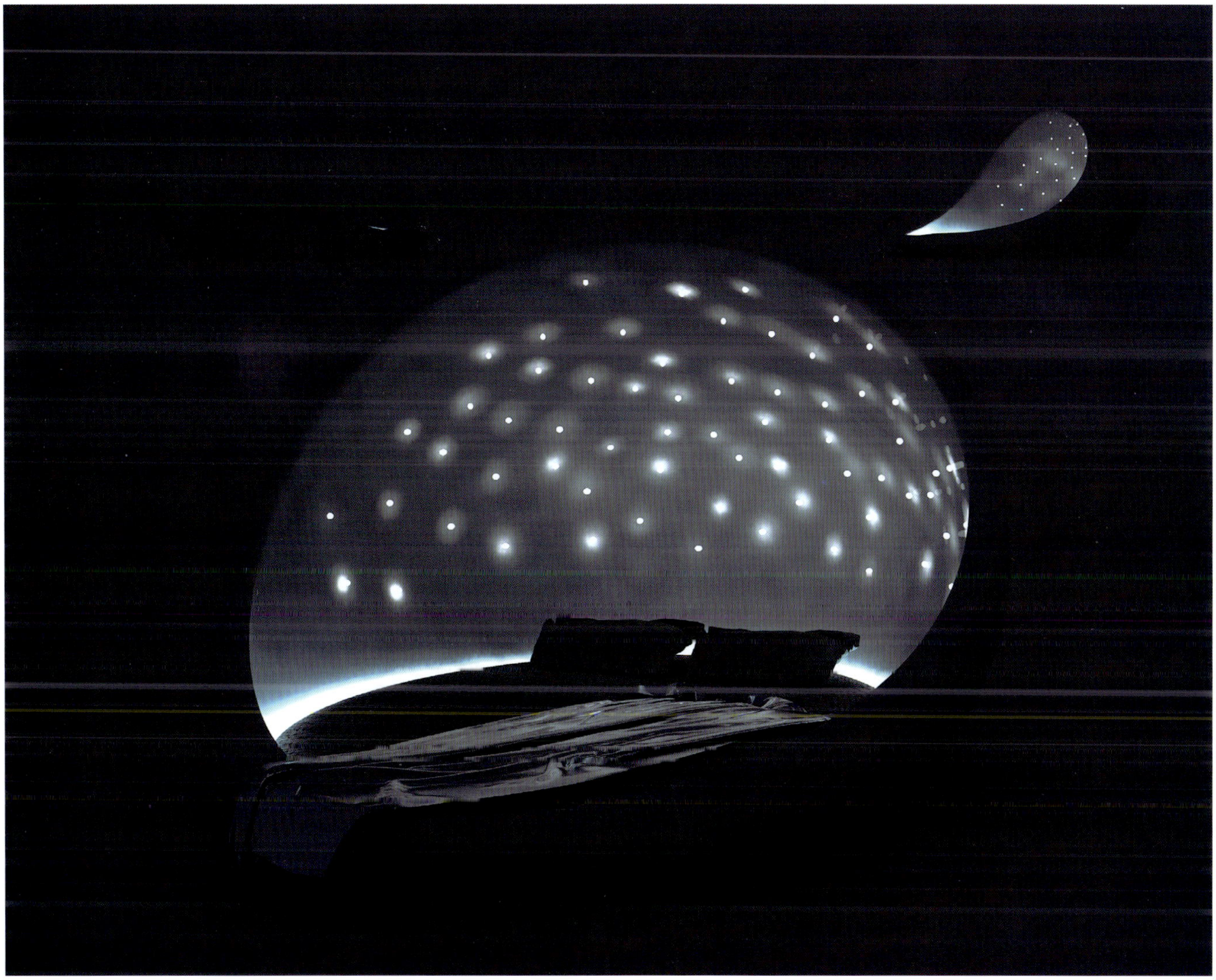

Luna

Studio Acorn Art Studio

Luna is intended to overcome the limits of conventional decoration and unveil the potential of a space. This hand-crafted moon lantern is mainly made of glass fiber and non-toxic latex, and is available in seven sizes. Its luminosity ranges from LUX1 to LUX5. Each piece comes with a cord for hanging it and a device to adjust luminosity.

Negative Ion Twig Lamp

Studio Design-Pie

This anion desk lamp is one solution to the increasing problem of indoor air pollution and computer radiation. 5 million anions are produced to purify the air and protect people from electromagnetic radiation, while providing a bright enough LED light. The infinity of nature has inspired the design team to make a greener indoor life. The leaves on the twig are individually touch-sensitive and are used to control the brightness of the light.

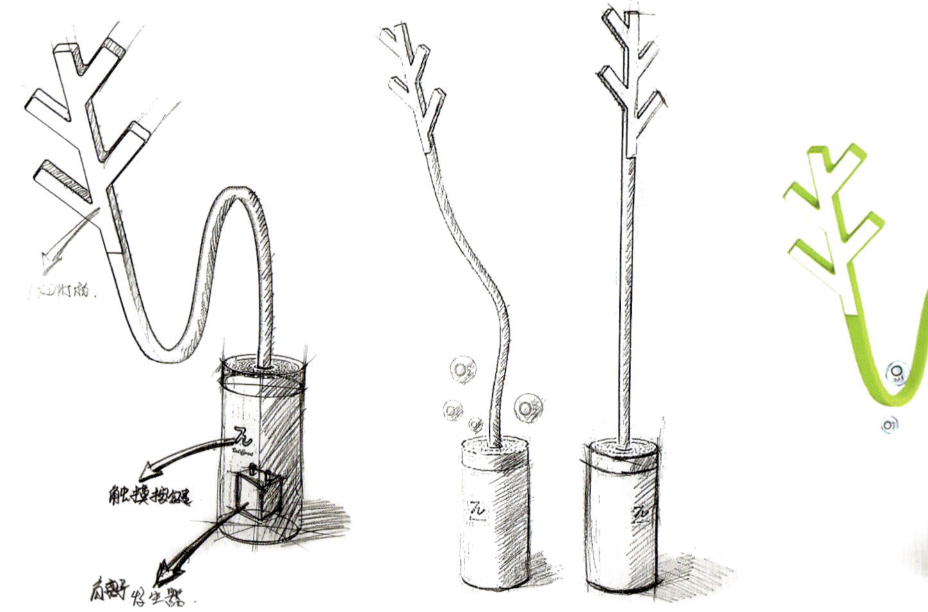

513MM
65MM

Streams of Sunlight

Designer Lisa Dudley

Inspired by the beams of light shining down through an opening in a cave, this design gives the experience of sunlight streaming into a space that would otherwise be untouched by the sun. Sunlight is collected via a parabolic reflector on the roof and then focused onto the ends of the fiber-optic cables. The light then travels down through the fiber-optic cables and enters the interior space through a recessed fixture in the ceiling. It is released just above the floor into a convex transparent dish, where the small points of light are magnified allowing the fluctuations of the natural environment to be observed through the changes in light.

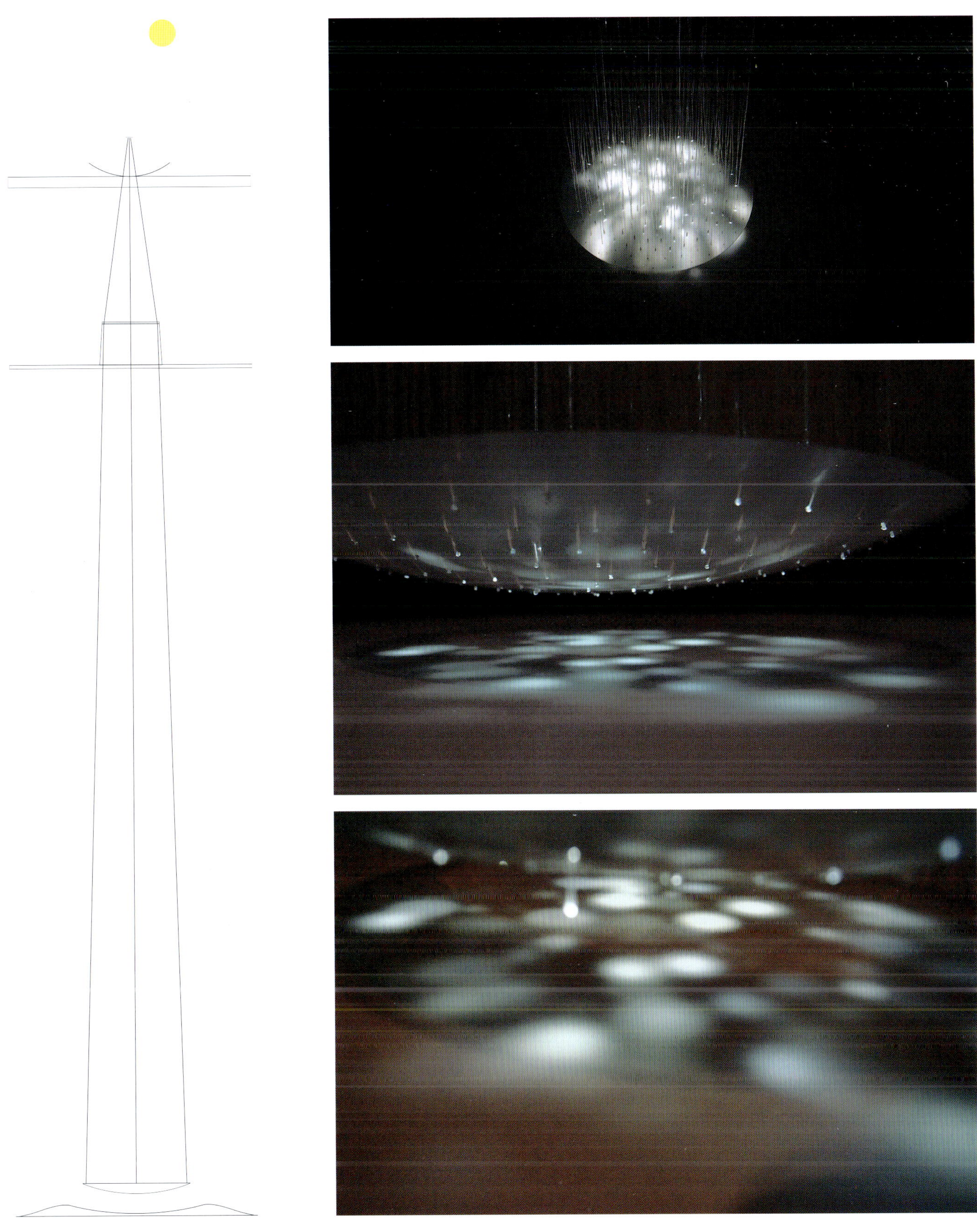

Function

Sofa So Good

Designer Janne Kyttanen

Sofa So Good is a full-size, fully functional lounger coated in high polish copper and chrome, 3D-printed in 6000 layers, each just 0.0099 centimeters thick. The lounger measures 150 x 75 x 55 cm, yet weighs only 2.5 kg and was created using just 2.5 liters of material. However, it can support up to 100 kg thanks to its unique diamond geometry, which is the result of observing silkworm cocoons and spider webs and applying their principles of structural optimization to manufacturing.

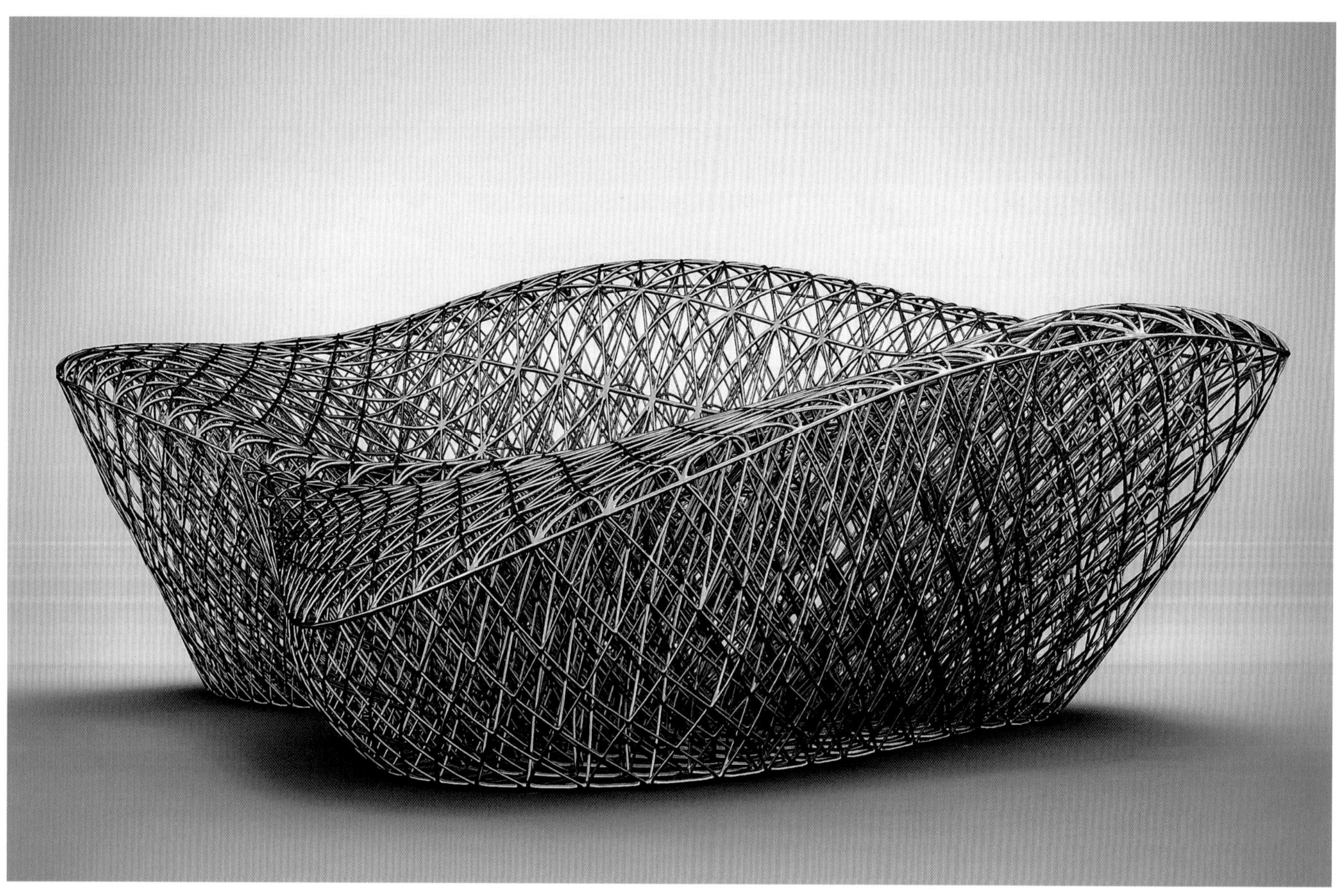

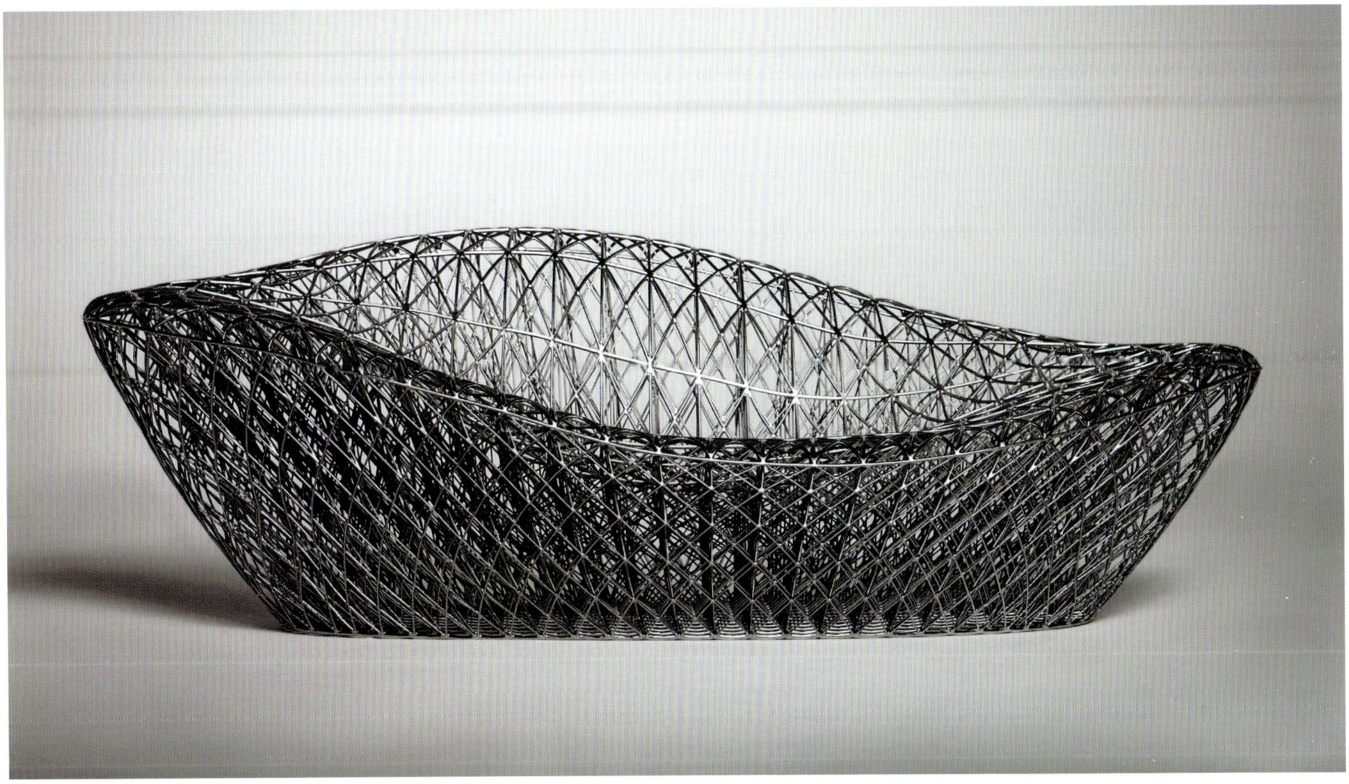

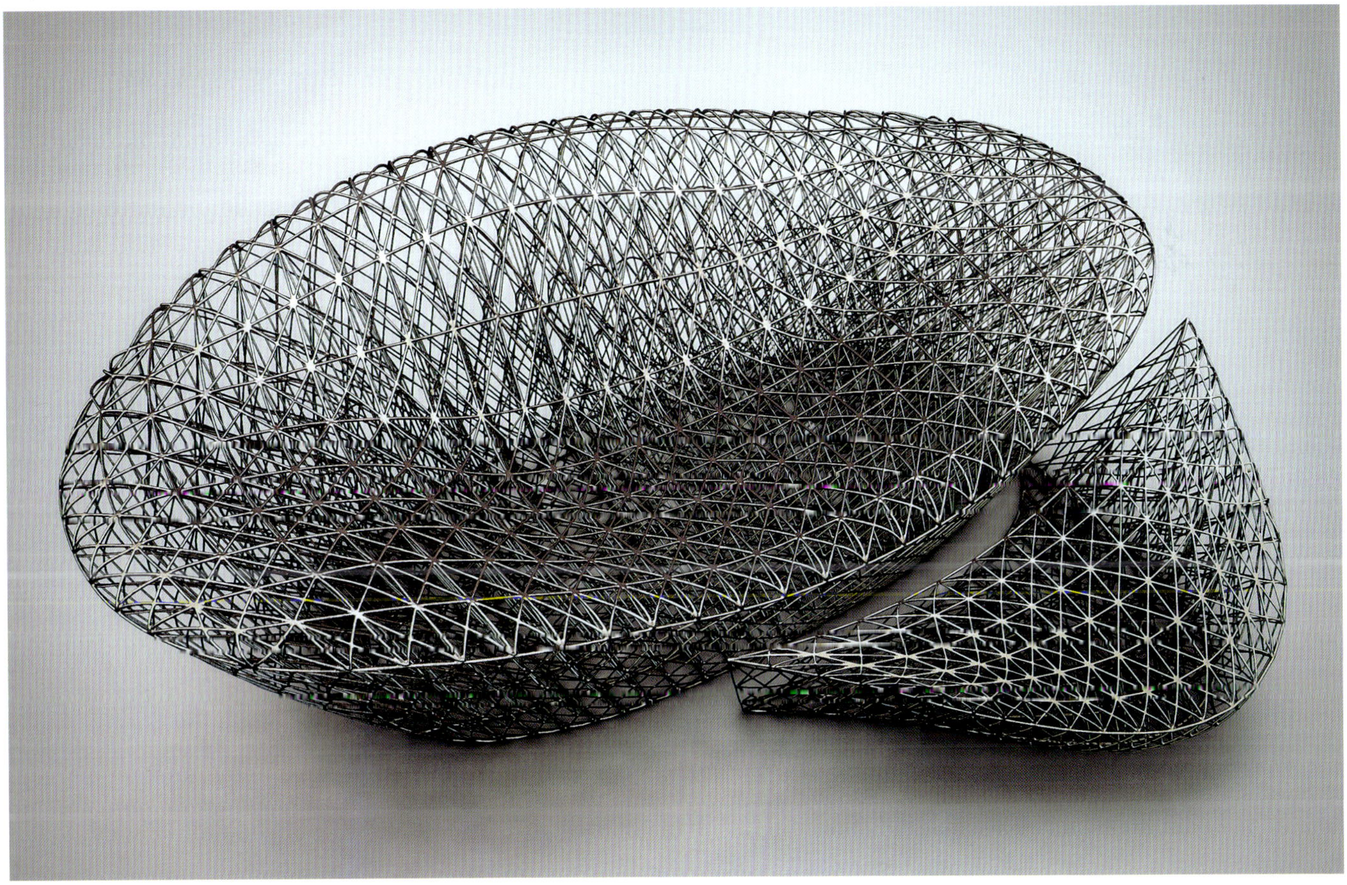

Scales

Studio MUT Design

Designer Alberto Sánchez

This series of ceramic wall tiles imitates the feeling of the vibrating movement of fish glistening under water. With the varied thickness of the tiles, and the fluorescent color of the edges shining on the smooth white surface, the assembled pieces produce an optical representation of the instant of motion.

Function

INDEX

Acknowledgements

We would like to thank all the designers and contributers who have been involved in the production of this book. Their contribution is indispensable in the compilation of this book. We would also like to express our gratitude to all the producers for their invaluable opinions and assistance throughout this project. And to the many others whose names are not credited but have made specific input in this book, we thank you for your continuous support.

FUTURE COOPERATIONS:
If you wish to participate in SendPoints' future projects and publications, please send your website or portfolio to editor01@sendpoints.cn